HSE
Health & Safety
Executive

IMPROVING COMPLIANCE WITH SAFETY PROCEDURES

Reducing industrial violations

HFRG

HSE BOOKS

The publication of this report is sponsored by the Health and Safety Executive. Its contents, and any opinions or conclusions expressed, are those of the authors alone, and do not necessarily reflect HSE policy. Any queries about the topics covered in this guide should be addressed to the authors, listed on page v, or to the Secretary of the Human Factors in Reliability Group (HFRG).

The blank tables in Appendix 2 may be freely copied.

CONTENTS

HUMAN FACTORS IN RELIABILITY GROUP (HFRG) VIOLATIONS SUB-GROUP

The Human Factors in Reliability Group (HFRG) is a forum for individuals from industry, regulatory and academic institutions who have an interest and expertise in human factors, associated with reliability. It was inaugurated in 1981 to foster collaboration between organisations with a direct interest in optimising and assessing human reliability in man-machine systems and to support research and dissemination of information in these areas. The main output from the HFRG has been the reports produced by the specialist sub-groups. This report has been produced by the Violations sub-group. Further information about the work of the HFRG can be obtained from the secretary at the SRD Association, Tel: 01952 254368.

Steve Mason (Chairman)   International Mining Consultants Ltd (IMCL)
                               PO Box 18, Huthwaite, Sutton-in-Ashfield,
                               Nottinghamshire NG17 2NS
                               Tel: 01623 441444 Fax: 01623 440333 Telex 37419 Mincon G

Becky Lawton (Née Free)   Department of Psychology
                               Oxford Road, University of Manchester M13 9PL
                               Tel: 0161 275 2600 Fax: 0161 275 2588

Vicki Travers   AEA Technology Consultancy Services (SRD)
                               Thomson House, Risley, Warrington, Cheshire WA3 6AT
                               Tel: 01925 254792 Fax: 01925 254538

Helen Rycraft   BNFL, Sellafield, B113, Seascale, Cumbria CA20 1PG
                               Tel: 01946 728833 Ext 75716 Fax: 09467 27056

Peter Ackroyd   Nuclear Electric plc Barnett Way, Barnwood,
                               Gloucester GL4 7RS
                               Tel: 01452 654129 Fax: 01452 654914

Steve Collier   Electrowatt Engineering Services (UK) Ltd
(Part-time member.   North Street, Horsham, West Sussex, RH12 1RF
 No longer with EES.)   Tel: 01403 250131 Fax: 01403 211899

The authors wish to thank the supporting organisations listed above and the following people who also gave their support: Peter Buckley (Health and Safety Executive), Stefka Charysyzn (Gloucester Health Authority), Prof Jim Reason (University of Manchester), Geoff Simpson (British Coal), Roger Taylor (British Rail), and Jerry Williams (Electrowatt).

ACKNOWLEDGEMENTS

The authors give special acknowledgement to the following specific contributions:

- The violation classification system used in the report was previously developed by Free during research carried out on the railway and previously developed by Prof Jim Reason in the book *Human Error*.

- The European Coal and Steel Community - Ergonomics Action Programme and British Coal for financial support for much of the production of the report and specifically for the development of the matrix approach for identifying solution avenues, and for many of the solution avenues.

- AEA Technology Consultancy Services and the Department of Psychology, University of Manchester for the development of the question set and solution avenues, and the Department of Psychology for the Interview section.

EXECUTIVE SUMMARY

Managers need to understand the underlying causes of human errors, and be aware of what they can do to reduce potential errors. Although attention has been given to the classification or quantification of inadvertent or accidental human errors made by operators, there has been little practical advice on how managers can successfully address deliberate breaches, or violations, of safety rules and procedures. But violations of safety procedures are a significant cause of many industrial accidents. Furthermore, violations are a frequent cause of production losses, poor quality and unreliable maintenance - with subsequent costs from poor reliability.

This report outlines practical strategies for reducing the potential for violations. It describes the role of violations in the wider context of human error. It summarises the nature of violations, and looks at the important factors that induce them. It shows how to identify violations and what measures to take to reduce or eliminate them.

The report shows how to identify violations by selecting rule sets which have the biggest risk for safety and/or production if they are not followed. A structured interview and questionnaire are then given to a selection of the workforce for each rule set. The results from these are used so management can identify which of the 13 solutions are most relevant to their wider potential violation problems. Management can develop detailed action plans to suit their specific problems from the suggestions offered.

INTRODUCTION TO HUMAN ERROR

1   There is often no tangible reward for working safely since it is difficult to appreciate an accident that has been avoided. There can, however, be no doubt that current safety programmes are preventing many accidents and as a result are saving industry an enormous amount of money in addition to the disruption, pain and suffering which occur as a result of accidents. If an industry is to continue to improve on its safety record, it must strive to reduce the potential for accidents, especially the potential for human failure.

2   Sir John Cullen recently emphasised management's responsibility for accident prevention by stating that 'lasting improvement in standards of health and safety can result only from effective and continuous effort initiated and controlled by management'. This applies just as much to human error as to physical agents. The Health and Safety Executive's (HSE) Accident Prevention Advisory Unit and others have shown that human error is a major contributory cause of 90% of accidents, 70% of which could have been prevented by management action.

3   Management must therefore be able to identify the potential hazards caused by human failure if they are to reduce behavioural accidents. This need was highlighted by John Rimington, the Director General of HSE, who said in his annual report for 1987/88 that 'a great many accidents happen through ignorance not only of proper precautions, but even of the existence of hazards'.

The costs of human error to industry

4   HSE estimates that the annual cost to UK industry from working unsafely is between £11 billion and £16 billion. Furthermore, it is estimated that most of these costs are uninsured – total accident costs are typically between eight and 36 times the insured costs. The effects of accident costs on industry can be crippling. One study has shown that the accident costs of one industry represented 14% of its potential output. In another industry these costs were shown to represent 37% of its profits, and in one construction company they represented 8% of its tender prices.

THE HERALD OF FREE ENTERPRISE INQUIRY

'All concerned in management, from the members of the Board of Directors down to the junior superintendents, were guilty of fault in that all must be regarded as sharing responsibility for the failure of management. From the top to the bottom the body corporate was infected with the disease of sloppiness.'

A reply from senior management to the Masters' requests for an on-bridge warning so incensed the Inquiry that the report quotes a number of replies verbatim, of which this is one:

'Do they need an indicator to tell them whether the deck storekeeper is awake and sober? My goodness!!'

The Inquiry indicated that because of delays at Dover, there was great pressure on crews to sail early. Memo from operations manager: '...put pressure on your first officer if you don't think he's moving fast enough...sailing late out of Zeebrugge isn't on. It's 15 minutes early for us.'

5   Losses of this scale are staggering and it is solely the responsibility of management to reduce these costs. Improvements in safety made by simply placing more emphasis on traditional approaches, such as the mandatory wearing of protective clothing or instigating

further engineering safeguards, are limited. John Rimington of HSE stresses that a good starting point would be to address the human component in accidents.

Increasing public concern over human error

6   In the past 10-15 years there has been an increasing interest in and recognition of the important contribution of human error to serious accidents. In particular, the accidents at Three Mile Island and Chernobyl focused attention on various types of human error and the need for improved ergonomics in the workplace. This interest has stimulated a more general appreciation of the importance of human errors and the recognition that they are major factors in personnel accident and injury, lost time and production.

7   Comments such as 'to err is human' can no longer be used as an excuse not to attempt to reduce the impact of human error on accidents, productivity and maintenance operations.

8   While most industries have gained a good reputation for controlling physical risks, few have applied the same attention to controlling the risks associated with human errors. The challenge, therefore, is for industries to achieve the same success in controlling the human risk to improve the overall safety of operations.

9   Most public awareness of human error until now has been of inadvertent or accidental errors made by operators. Traditionally, the phrase 'human error' has been restricted to those with 'hands-on' control of, or influence on, of equipment immediately before the accident, and has had connotations of individual blame and responsibility. This narrow view, restricted to operator error, has provided only a partial approach to accident prevention.

10   Most accidents involve a chain of events and often involve the earlier decisions or actions of senior management. A successful approach to reducing the potential for human error should therefore look at the risks of error at all stages of an organisation.

11   The King's Cross Inquiry almost totally absolves everyone on site on the night of the disaster from any significant share of the responsibility for the incident. Primary responsibility is placed squarely on the organisation and management for inaction and ineffectiveness in relation to safety standards.

12   Tragedies such as the loss of the Challenger space shuttle and Chernobyl stimulate similar recognition of the impact of management and organisational issues.

13   Despite this growing interest violations is a class of human error that has largely escaped public and management attention although it is one of the most significant types of error in terms of its contribution to accidents and lost production.

THE EFFECT OF VIOLATIONS ON SAFETY AND EFFICIENCY

What are violations?

14   Violations are any deliberate deviations from the rules, procedures, instructions and regulations drawn up for the safe or efficient operation and maintenance of plant or equipment. Breaches in these rules could be accidental, unintentional or deliberate. This report is concerned with identifying and reducing deliberate breaches of rules and procedures.

15   Violations occur for many reasons, and are seldom wilful acts of sabotage or vandalism. Most stem from a genuine desire to perform work satisfactorily given the constraints and expectations that exist. The signalling wiring errors associated with the Clapham junction disaster

(Department of Transport, 1988) provided an extreme example of both the significance of this type of failure, and the extent to which violations or deviations from laid down procedures can become the norm within an organisation.

16 It should be noted that violations are frequently called, or include, circumventions in the USA.

The extent of violations

17 Much evidence suggests that violations occur frequently both at work and in general life. Car driving shows a variety of differing types of violation, eg drink driving, speeding, jumping traffic lights. Failure to obey public notices such as 'No Smoking', 'Do not walk on the grass', 'No Parking' clearly shows that violations are commonplace.

18   In the workplace, there is also widespread evidence of a high level of routine violations. Many accidents and injuries arise partially or wholly through various violations, such as removing guards on machinery. Some recent disasters have highlighted the degree to which violations can become the normal way of working, eg the work practices and lack of supervision involved in the Clapham tragedy.

19   Violations have not been identified systematically in most incident reports, because of their often controversial nature. Thus, the hard evidence of accident statistics doesn't help. However, there is enough information from particular investigations to suggest that they are a very significant type of human error. Given that human errors underlie 70-90% of accidents and injuries (HSE Accident Prevention Advisory Unit), violations are an important contributor to industry's risks and costs.

The significance of violations

20 If violations are relatively common, are they significant in terms of their undesirable effects? The examples quoted of violations in both general life and in the workplace immediately indicate the impact of violations on accidents and injuries.

21   The safety impact of violations is relatively easy to see from the available evidence but, as with most other forms of human failure, there are other less obvious impacts. These include the effects on lost production and output, and the immediate effects arising from the safety impacts in terms of compensation payments, lost time through injuries, plant damage etc.

22   The additional costs caused by violations can be considerable, but management and employees are often unaware of this. This lack of awareness can itself increase the potential for violations and mean that management overlook problems even with easy remedies.

23   It is therefore difficult to quantify or estimate the full impact of the effects of violations, but they are likely to be considerable. Thus, the benefits of reducing violations will include safety, productivity and equipment reliability.

THE MANAGEMENT ROLE

24   Violations are highly susceptible to management influence as most underlying causes of violations are either created by management, accepted by management or condoned as normal working practice by management neglect.

25   Very often, a workforce believes that management would 'pressure' them to perform jobs more quickly - this belief being based, in part, on the evidence of management apparently turning a blind eye to any improvised methods. This could have been because management did not notice such improvisation, or management pressures may be real, rather than perceived. As a result, in many workplaces, violations have become the normal methods of working, rather than the laid down procedures. Not surprisingly these breaches in rules eventually lead to incidents.

26   An easy management response to an incident may be a hasty introduction or revision of rules and procedures, perhaps without consideration of the full practical implications. Such a response might have more to do with

reinforcing the management's position, than with fully discharging their responsibilities for safety.

27 Furthermore, with the trend towards more flexible working, rules and procedures may need to be revised for the new regimes.

28 The motives for any violation may be specific to the individual or may be generalised across a work group. Simple universal solutions are unlikely, but management have a variety of 'tools' at their disposal which they can apply to specific potential violations once they become apparent. Many of these measures can be surprisingly easy to apply.

Solutions

29   The solutions open to management for reducing violation potential are improvements to design, training, supervision/management, and organisation. The exact type of solution chosen will depend on the specific contributory factors identified as potentially important. Some

actions would be directed at the workforce while others would need to be directed at management or the organisation. For example a poor perception of the safety risks associated with a task is clearly a factor internal to an individual. Pressure from management is clearly an external influence. The action routes are therefore different. For example training the individual may address their poor perception of safety risks. Pressure from management, however, would involve management training as well as other actions.

30 Detailed examples of typical management actions are covered in the section on 'Methodology'.

31   A first step towards reducing the potential for industrial violations is to gain a better understanding of the reasons or motives which lie behind specific violations. Then, the most effective way of dealing with them will become clear. To achieve this a classification system has been devised.

The need to classify violations

32   Several detailed classification systems have been developed to try to obtain a deeper understanding of the nature of violations. If, however, we are only interested in assessing a work process to identify important potential violations and then to identify the most likely effective action routes to reduce or eliminate them, a simpler approach can be adopted.

33   Violations can be classified as routine violations, situational violations, exceptional violations and optimising violations.

Routine violations

34   A routine violation is a behaviour in opposition to the rule, procedure or instruction that has become the normal way of behaving within the person's peer/work group. The violating behaviour is normally automatic and unconscious. The violation is recognised as such by the individual, if questioned.

IMPRACTICAL RULES ENCOURAGE VIOLATIONS

A Code of Practice stated that no person should enter a bunker or silo unless all material adhering to the bunker sides had been removed above the point where the work had to be performed. This was a requirement to prevent vibration etc causing adhering material to fall on the people working below - a known cause of fatal accidents. Despite the obvious importance of this requirement men were still being killed in this way. When this was investigated it became apparent that there was no practical way of fullfilling the Code of Practice requirement. Workers chose to take the risk to get the job done.

35   Violations become routine within a work group as a result of a number of factors:

- Cutting corners, saving time and energy are basic human instincts. Behind every sign which reads 'Do not walk across the grass' no doubt lies a well-trodden path across that very plot.

- Where rules are perceived as overly restrictive, skilled individuals may think they can violate the rules with little risk to their safety, and the resulting violations are likely to become routine. For the reasons above, the routine violations are rarely restricted to a particular group, but tend to be rife throughout the organisation, industry or population.

- Such violations may be due to a belief that the rules are no longer applicable. This type of violation can

ACCIDENT INQUIRIES INTO FATAL MINING ACCIDENTS

'I am aware of men riding the conveyor and have seen them doing so since legal man-riding was discontinued .... but none have been caught by a District Overman or Deputy as far as I am aware ....' (Despite the fact that he was the district deputy!)

'I have signed for and read the Support Rules but I cannot remember what they said ...' (District official)

'I have been issued with, and signed for, copies of the Manager's Support Rules ... I have read them and fully understood their content ... I was aware that the Support Rules were not being adhered to ... however in my opinion no additional support was required ...' (Contractor's official)

frequently occur where employees see little value in the original rule and there is insufficient management commitment. Management needs to explain the reasons behind the rule or to change the rule if it becomes inappropriate.

- Routine violations are commonly associated with a lack of enforcement of the rule. The individual is unlikely to be reprimanded or even caught violating the rule. In Holland, for example, about 70% of the cycling population ignore red traffic lights. There are so many traffic lights, that stopping at every one would greatly increase travelling time. There is very little chance of being caught for violating this traffic law, thus it has become the social norm. Speeding is another example.

36 Routine violations can be minimised by:

- assessing the risks and reducing risk-taking behaviour;

- increasing the probability of detection;

- rationalising the work systems to reduce the numbers of unnecessary rules.

ELECTRICIAN FAILS TO ADOPT PROCEDURES FOR LIVE JOINTING OF CABLES

Work was programmed to carry out a live cut of a cable and reterminate to a new cable. The jointer was later found shaking with the live end of the cable in his hand. He was pulled clear but could not be revived. The jointer had no rubber gloves with him at the termination and had no clothes above his waist. It is believed that he had his bare back against a brick wall. Both live and neutral/earth conductors were exposed with no shrouding.

The Board of Inquiry concluded that the jointer was at fault for not using rubber gloves, being improperly dressed and for baring more than one conductor at once.

Situational violations

37 These violations occur because of factors dictated by the employees' immediate work space or environment. These include the design and condition of the work area, time pressure, number of staff, supervision, equipment availability and design, and factors outside the organisation's control, such as weather and time of day.

RULE EROSION AND IMPROVISED TOOL LED TO FATALITY

The rules of a plant required a boiler to be completely isolated from the rest of the steam generating plant before men entered it. It seemed that men first entered the boiler without complete isolation when it was thought essential to get a boiler back on line with the minimum of delay. Since everything went satisfactorily, the same procedure had apparently been adopted again, even when there was no particular hurry. Gradually, therefore, the importance of the correct procedure had been forgotten or eroded and on several occasions complete reliance had been placed on the presence and reliability of a boiler fitter and his keys.

Boilers are periodically 'blown-down' to reduce the level of contaminants in the boiler water. The super-heated boiler water flashes into steam as it is discharged through a manifold into a blow-down drum.

The blow-down valves were operated by a special key which had a lug on it so that it could not be removed when the valve was open. It was therefore impossible, in theory, for the blow-down valves from two boilers to be opened together. However the boiler fitter 'kept and jealously guarded' a private key without a lug and had used it to open the blow-down valve on the boiler that was under repair. When the operating boiler was blown-down steam entered the boiler under repair through the common manifold and a man was killed.

38   These violations often occur when a rule is impossible or extremely difficult to work to in a particular situation. There may be conflicting requirements or it may be physically impossible to perform the activities in the specified manner. Personnel performing the activities have to violate some aspects of the rules or procedures to achieve the end requirement. It may even be the case that working to the rule in these circumstances is, or is perceived to be, unsafe.

39   The rejection of such safety rules usually occurs because the rule or procedure is perceived to be inappropriate or ineffective for the situation, or there are considerable benefits perceived from an alternative action. The reasons for such rejections can be both well motivated, eg an alternative action is seen as being potentially safer, or gives benefits to the company; or can be for purely personal gain, eg deliberate risk-taking to eliminate extra work, or to gain status with work colleagues.

40   In addition, supervision and management are likely to ignore many of these violations because the job would suffer from strict compliance. Operational difficulties which arise from working strictly to the rules are usually ample proof that the systems for developing and implementing safety rules and procedures are seriously flawed.

41   Situational violations will vary to some extent from plant to plant, depot to depot etc, because the nature of the situation is differerent.

42   These violations indirectly lead to other violations. If people feel that they have to violate the rules in particular situations, they may not comply with other rules, less restricted by situation, because rules in general command less respect.

43   A situational violation may become routine if the circumstances producing the violation are constant. However, for the purposes of finding solutions, the two categories are distinct.

DISABLED DOOR INTERLOCK

The access to a hazardous area was via a cascade keying system whereby the system kept keys captive to prevent access and the initiating key was kept by the supervisor. This key could only be turned when the various sensors indicated that the conditions were safe within the area. This key released a captive key to open the area's door. As the lock on the door had been changed, the new key was welded on the ring of the captive key to maintain the interlock.

One day some workers required access into the hazardous area but the first key would not turn. Checks confirmed that there were no hazards in the area and so it was concluded that the interlock was faulty. In order to gain access the keys were separated.

The faulty interlock was not reported as per instruction. The separation of the keys was not recorded or authorised and the personnel making access did not comply with three written procedures for the control of access via a permit-to-work system. The interlock continued to be overridden for some time with failure of planned maintenance due to poor communication.

OIL RIG EXPLOSION RAISES NEW NORTH SEA PLATFORM QUESTIONS

Following an incident inquiry on an oil platform, a report identified the presence of over 1500 electrical system faults on the platform. The company confirmed that the report was accurate but said that the apparently high total was misleading as many were minor and relate to faulty labelling or missing screws.

A specialist said that in his view such a degree of electrical faults would require a thorough investigation of the planned maintenance systems. He questioned the maintenance procedures and structure of supervisory arrangements both offshore and onshore that would have led to a build-up of so many faults.

44   Situational violations can be often be overcome by:

- improved job design;

- improved hazard reporting systems;

- improved working conditions;

- more appropriate supervision.

Exceptional violations

45   These are violations that are rare and happen only in particular circumstances, often when something goes wrong. They occur to a large extent when an individual is attempting to solve problems in unusual situations. The individual, in attempting to solve new problems, violates a rule to achieve the desired goal. These violations are commonly associated with high risk, often because the consequences of the action are not fully understood or because the violation is known to be dangerous but seems inescapable.

46   Typical solutions for addressing exceptional violations would be to:

- increase training for unusual situations;

- reduce pressure on individuals to react quickly and provide support so they can cope with such situations;

- ensure 'defences' are in place to prevent such violations resulting in accidents.

Optimising violations

47   A final class of violations is created by a motive to optimise a work situation. These violations are usually caused through:

- a need for excitement in jobs which are considered repetitive, unchallenging or boring;

- a desire to explore the boundaries of a system which are thought to be too restrictive;

- pure inquisitiveness.

48   Optimising violations can be reduced through a process of job redesign and an examination of rules which are considered restrictive.

General factors

49   There is a general tendency for violations to become routine because most violations involve less time and effort. A number of forces push and pull to establish a particular level of violation. Some of these general factors are illustrated below.

- Research has indicated that time pressure, high work load and the need to do the job more quickly increase the likelihood of all types of violation occurring. These factors are also particularly significant in producing other forms of error.

CHERNOBYL
Having been released from the grid, the operators continued power reduction. A further operator failure led to very low power. At this point, analysts agree the test should have been abandoned in view of the dangerously low power settings. Operators and engineers, however, continued to improvise in an unfamiliar and increasingly unstable regime to protect the test plan. The plant later went super prompt critical.

- There will be many situations where there is a conscious balancing of the perceived risks of alternative actions against the perceived benefits, eg reduced workload, shorter times, higher output etc. Although the rule or procedure is known, there appear to be alternatives that offer greater benefits with an acceptable level of perceived risk. Unfortunately the actual levels of risk can be very different from the perceived ones. Typical examples of this type of violation are workers not using protective equipment as it slows down their work, affects their earnings etc.

- Another type of risk-taking is where individuals become complacent or over-familiar with the process or operations they are performing and take short cuts to either create additional interest or excitement in their work, or to gain some level of perceived kudos from their peers. This type of violation is probably rare.

- Organisational culture is an important factor, although difficult to research objectively and for which the introduction of changes is a lengthy process. Most organisations have safety as their first stated goal, however it could sometimes appear that in reality production is the first concern.

- The work to rule, which is used as a form of industrial action, demonstrates that the colloquial 'rules are there to be broken' is not a myth formulated by lazy workers. When workers feel that the company wants them to break or bend rules, any efforts by the company to increase safety by reducing violations tends to be seen as merely protecting management's position.

- Rules themselves can increase the likelihood to violate. In older industries, rules are extremely prescriptive. In many cases they arise from past accidents. Gradually action has been regulated to a greater and greater extent. Action required to do the job does not narrow to the same extent, forcing people to stray outside the regulated area. Increased restriction of behaviour reduces the skills needed for the job. People feel they have become automatons and pride in their job disappears. There is a reaction against this, most predominantly within the older population of workers, who have seen skill taken away from them.

- Accidents are often by their very nature unpredictable. A rule may be inappropriate because it is written to prevent a specific accident occurring again, for which the chance is extremely small. As a result, rules perceived as overly restrictive because of the minimal risk associated with them may be given as much emphasis as a rule which is indispensable.

- Enforcement is also important. Few companies and industries can afford the level of supervision required to enforce all the necessary rules. Often supervisors and managers differentiate between those rules for which compliance is paramount and those which can be ignored. When managers and supervisors ignore some violations, the employees may feel their actions are condoned.

BASIC STRATEGIES FOR REDUCING VIOLATION POTENTIAL

50   Despite the significance of violations for the accident potential of an organisation, there has been surprisingly little systematic effort directed to the identification and reduction of this form of human error. Previous HFRG guidance reports (eg HFRG, 1991) have addressed some of the factors likely to encourage violations, however these have tended to concentrate on the reduction of inadvertent human failings.

51   Traditional accident investigations tended to concentrate on the technical issues, and on the identification of blame, and the recommendations tended to be vague and largely ineffective when concerned with reducing violations. Recommendations included providing more training, taking disciplinary action, telling individuals to take more care, revising procedures etc. For example although training is one of the key routes to reducing violations, such empty recommendations will rarely help the training manager to effectively revise the content of any courses.

52   An improved methodology is therefore needed, preferably one which has been produced specifically to address violations.

53   Whenever a person is faced with unfavourable conditions or circumstances (eg pain, discomfort, socio-economic problems) it is natural for that person to seek to develop alternative strategies for coping with them. At the most basic level a poorly designed or located control will cause discomfort or annoyance and it is likely that the operators will attempt to reduce their inconvenience. For example a common response to a poorly designed deadman pedal is to jam the pedal down. At a higher level, an operator may find there are several safety rules which, in certain circumstances, conflict with one another. To achieve an operational goal the operator may then have to choose which rule to break.

INCIDENT RELEASING HYDROGEN FLUORIDE FUME

During a routine transfer of concentrated hydrofluoric acid from a storage tank to a mobile tanker, a chargehand noticed an abnormal pressure build up in the mobile tanker. He immediately stopped the transfer operations and found that both of the flexible connectors joining the mobile tanker to the fixed pipework from the storage tank were badly kinked. He reported this to the plant foreman.

Having released the excess pressure to the scrubber, the foreman asked for the mobile tanker to be moved under his supervision, despite this being in direct contravention of the operating instructions for this section of the plant.

The movement caused a valve to fracture and a small amount of hydrogen fl120ride fume to be released.

54   An important point to remember is that whenever an individual decides to violate rules or procedures, the task can often change from one which is routinely faced to one where at least certain aspects are novel. Such work could then require knowledge based skills (Rasmussen, 1987) where the individual is relying on his or her own understanding of the system. This can lead to new types of error.

55   In another example, the violation could be for a driver to shoot a red traffic light. The reason behind this violation could be that he/she was changing channel on the car radio and simply didn't notice the lights changing, or it could be that the driver was late for a programme he/she wanted to see on television and deliberately decided to risk overshooting the red light. In both cases the driver broke the rule and the safety consequences would be the same. However in the first example it is clear that the traffic offence was not a deliberate act by the driver and would therefore fall outside the remit of this report. In terms of human error classification it would be an inadvertent error caused by a lapse of attention. You must therefore distinguish between deliberate acts which contravene rules or codes of practices and inadvertent rule breaking which occurs as a result of mistakes or slips.

56   In both examples, the motives behind the violations are clearly very different and the best remedial solutions would also be different for each case.

Towards a solution

57   An insight into the most appropriate routes for eliminating or reducing the potential for violations lies in a deeper understanding of the basic motives behind the violation. As discussed earlier these can be numerous and varied, and often combined together.

58   The exact combination of motives behind any violation is likely to be specific to the individual and complex in nature. Although various classification systems have been devised to address the complex motives which lie behind many violations, we need not be overly concerned with these if our objective is simply to identify and reduce the likelihood of potential violations in a work setting. This is because many of these basic motives to violate are a reflection of an individual's attitude and it is increasingly accepted that it is difficult and unpredictable to attempt to change these attitudes directly. It is more effective to change the factors which influence these attitudes, ie the organisational, training, management and supervision, job design and equipment design factors which are present in the working environment. We need not therefore address the prime motivating factors directly.

59   There are a number of avenues open to management to systematically reduce the potential for violations. The exact response to changes in any of these factors can, however, never be reliably predicted as it will be shaped by personal criteria. Any fixed solutions will therefore, by definition, have variable effects and any desired results may or may not be achieved in practice. Even if they are proved to have had some success, the effect may not have been as great as was envisaged. A vital part of reducing the potential for violation is therefore effecitve monitoring. Without this feedback management can never be sure they are achieving the desired end result.

60   Some general purpose methodologies have recently been developed which help analysts investigate incidents involving human errors, including violations. However, these are only likely to be effective when used by human factors specialists and they only aim to identify the critical factors in the chain of events which have led to an actual incident. A problem with this approach is that it is reactive and the 'latent failings' (Reason, 1990) identified are specific to the incident which is being assessed. Any response will therefore only be aimed at reducing the probability of a similar incident.

Reactive or proactive safety management?

61   Managers need not wait until there is an incident involving a violation before they act to reduce the likelihood of a repeat incident. It is suggested that a better approach is to conduct an audit of potential violations in a work environment.

62   The outcome is a profile of organisation factors which can be seen to increase the potential for violations. In this proactive approach any remedial changes made by management will address the wider influences identified in the organisation, rather than those relating to a specific incident.

63   As the organisational factors identified would probably be influential in a wider range of potential violations, the resulting remedial actions would be more effective and wide ranging than any identified from an investigation of a small number of incidents.

64   Therefore although the approach described in this report could be used as part of an accident investigation, it is offered as a methodology which can be used as part of a regular and systematic safety audit of a company, or as part of commissioning exercises on a new plant or machinery.

65   This approach also recognises the ineffectiveness of some audits of behaviour which involve observations of staff at work once every six months or every year, where it is difficult to uncover a true picture.

THE HFRG VIOLATION APPROACH

66   This report offers a methodology which can be used easily by non-specialists to identify potentially critical violation risks in any work organisation and to suggest basic remedial routes which they should consider. Although the information in this report should enable non-skilled assessors to carry out suitable assessments, further advice and guidance can be obtained from human factors specialists. The HFRG approach offers a means to identify the important organisational factors and the most appropriate solutions quickly.

67   The potential violation assessment can be undertaken:

•   at the commissioning stages of plant;

•   as part of an accident investigation;

•   as part of a routine human error audit;

•   as part of risk awareness or risk assessments.

It is recommended that this exercise should be complemented by a wider assessment of the potential for other significant human errors.

Objectives

68   When developing the HFRG violations approach the following objectives were arrived at.

- The methodology should be capable of identifying the range of underlying background or organisation factors which could work independently or in combination to increase the likelihood of violations. These factors have been termed 'latent failings' (Reason, 1990).

- The assessment need only identify the presence of the latent failures to direct management towards actions which eliminate or reduce the effect of these failings. The potential violations themselves need not be formally identified.

- The methodology should be capable of being used for high frequency (known) violations as well as potential violations.

- It should be able to identify the more critical rules within an organisation which warrant detailed attention.

- The checklists (or similar) would be completed by the line managers and/or the workforce as appropriate.

- The methodology should enable management to establish any priorities for action.

- The methodology should provide guidance to enable management to develop detailed strategies for action based on their own specific needs.

Overview of methodology

69   The methodology begins by selecting the rules and procedures which cause the most concern for safety and/or production if they are not followed. In addition a structured interview is conducted on a selection of the workforce to identify long-term 'safety culture' issues. Each of these important rules is also assessed using a checklist. A small sample of the workforce is asked to rate the degree to which they agree with a number of statements. Depending on their response, each statement receives a score. Four simple scoring methods are then used to collate the scores of the workforce.

70   These scores are then entered into a matrix. The matrix identifies which of 13 generic solution avenues would be applicable for minimising the violation potential in the organisation. A further simple scoring method is then used to select the best generic solutions for each important rule set. These can then be compared across the other important rule sets being investigated and management can then identify those most relevant to their potential violation problems.

71   Each generic solution avenue is then expanded to give a number of suggestions or guidelines from which organisations can select the most relevant. These can then be developed by management into a specific action plan tailored to the particular organisation.

72   The methodology is described in four stages:

- identifying the main problems (para 73);

- understanding the causes of the problem (para 79);

- identifying potential routes to solutions (para 97);

- selecting appropriate solution avenues (para 100).

IDENTIFYING THE MAIN PROBLEMS

73   Management determine the most important sets of rules and procedures to the company on safety and/or quality of product or service. This means they are applying the methodology to areas where violations would have the largest effect on the company. This step ensures that the methodology is both quick and effective to apply. The procedure can be applied later to remaining rule sets, if necessary.

Selecting rule sets

74   The selection of critical rule sets can be done in one of two ways:

(a)   from an initial list of generalised rules and procedures, management are asked to add rules wherever necessary and then to simply judge the list to pick out the 5 to 10 (say) rules which would give them the biggest concern should they be broken in any way;

(b)   this selection process can be refined if necessary, by an approach which is based on a risk assessment.

75   If management are solely concerned with safety, the critical rule sets would be selected from the organisation's safety rules and procedures - many of which will have relevance to both safety and production/quality. Other critical rule sets will relate to products/service quality and will have no relevance to safety. For example it is possible that a rule violation could lead to the rejection of a batch of product because it caused poor quality.

76   This stage is therefore restricted to the identification of the rule sets with the largest potential consequences should they be broken. In effect, this top listing is equivalent to a consequences rating for each set of rules and procedures.

77   The complete listing of rule sets is then given to a selection of the workforce, who are also asked to select those they think are potentially the most important to the company's well-being (safety and/or quality/service).

78   Both sets of top selections (management's and the workforce's) are then scrutinised.

(a)   Where there is unaminous agreement, the most critical rule sets are selected for more detailed assessment.

(b)   Where there are discrepancies between the sets selected by management and the workforce this may indicate that the rules need reviewing in the light of practical experience. However, it could indicate that the workforce underestimate the importance of certain rule sets and may need extra training directed specifically at enhancing their understanding of the risks associated with not following those rules. After due consideration management should select the rule sets to be assessed.

(c)   Where there is unanimous agreement that certain rule sets contribute little to the company's well-being, then the recommendation is to analyse whether or not they are necessary.

UNDERSTANDING THE CAUSES OF THE PROBLEM

79   An interview section is used here to determine any necessary longer-term cultural and organisational changes. A checklist/matrix methodology supplements the interview and is primarily aimed at identifying shorter to medium-term solutions. The practitioner should therefore aim to use both parts of the procedure. Remember that lasting improvements can often only be sustained by long-term cultural changes.

The interview

80   A structured interview is given to a selection of the workforce and management. The interview, which is described in Appendix 3, is aimed at identifying the longer-term organisational and safety culture issues. It is used with the checklists to obtain a management strategy (short and long-term solutions) for reducing the potential for violations.

Table 1 Outline for the interview

	Area	Appropriate solution
1	Responsibility for safety	Safety commitment - workforce
2	Rule enforcement and management responsibility	Safety commitment - management
3	Analysing accidents and developing improvements	Rules and procedures - design and application
		Organisation
4	Complexity or ambiguity of rules	Rules and procedures - design and application
5	Safety vs production conflict	Supervision - monitoring and detection
		Safety commitment - management organisation
6	Violations with serious consequences – why?	Organisation
		Supervision - monitoring and detection
7	Purpose of rules	Rules and procedures - design
		Safety commitment - management
		Organisation
8	Doing jobs not trained for	Training - rules and procedures
		Training - hazards and risks
		Logistics support
		Job design
9	Hazards in the work place (improvements required)	Work conditions
		Plant and equipment design and modifications
10	Rewarding safe practice (means for)	Logistic support
		Organisation
		Supervision - monitoring and detection

81   The basic outline of the interview is given in Table 1.

82   The interview also provides an opportunity for staff to air their views on the organisational culture in relation to rules and safety. Responses provide an insight into the attitudes which pervade the organisation and can affect the level of compliance in general.

83   Such insights are likely to be invaluable to management when attempting to apply the solution strategies identified by the audit questionnaire. It is important to ensure that remideal actions are not at odds with the organisational culture.

The checklist

84   The violation classification has been used to generate a comprehensive question set which identifies the more important factors in any organisation which could promote violations. An example of a completed individual checklist is shown in Table 2, along with the analysis charts to be used for each of the rule sets being investigated.

Completing the checklist

85   For each of the rule sets selected, a representative sample of the workforce is invited to complete the questionnaire. By restricting each question to a specific rule set (eg rules and procedures associated with electrical safety), each question will be more meaningful and easier to answer. Normally a minimum of 15 people should examine each generic rule set, however if the workforce is smaller the whole workforce should be questioned.

86   The responses to each statement will be of the form: ... if the potential problem applies to the specific rule set, to what degree do you agree with the statement?

87   For example, the statement could be, 'I have (electrical safety) rules for tasks I will never have to do', if yes: state whether you agree slightly, agree, or strongly agree. Another statement could be, 'Supervisors seldom discipline workers who break rules'.

Scoring the questionnaire

88   In this way, for each rule set, the subjects will be asked to rate the degree to which they agree with each of 48 statements given in the questionnaire.

89   If subjects disagree with a statement/question a 0 is entered in the column to the right of the statement.

90   If subjects agree with the statement they will be asked whether they agree slightly, agree, or strongly agree with the statement. Depending on the answer, each question would be allocated a score of 1, 3 or 6 respectively. This is entered in the score column adjacent to the statement.

91   An example of a questionnaire is shown in Table 2 for a single plant operator.

92   Using the following procedure will give a good indication of the most appropriate management action.

Scoring system

93   The scores against each statement are first collated using the chart shown in Table 3. This shows an example from a study based on ten completed questionnaires. For example, 6 of the 10 subjects agreed, or strongly agreed, with the first statement.

94   By allocating scores of 1 for every 'slightly agree', 3 for every 'agree' and 6 for every 'strongly agree' a total score can be obtained. These scores are entered in Column A in Table 4.

95   It is possible that no entries will be made against a statement as all subjects may disagree with it. The number of entries (whether a 1, 3 or 6) gives a separate indication of potential magnitude of the problem. For example, a statement is more likely to be a factor increasing the violation potential if 7 out of 10 subjects agree with it than if only 2 agree with it. The number of entries against each statement is therefore taken from Table 3 and entered into Column B of Table 4.

96   A further indication of 'strength' of the relevance of each statement is the number of subjects giving full mark, or 6, scores. Again these are easily taken from Table 3 and entered into Column C.

IDENTIFYING POTENTIAL ROUTES TO SOLUTIONS

97   Using this scoring system management can obtain an indication of which solution avenues would be most appropriate for the specific pattern of organisational factors increasing the potential for violation.

98   Consider only those solution avenues with the largest scores initially. Management may then need to study only three or four solution avenues which are determined from the following selection procedures. Although other solutions would inevitably have some relevance, this procedure focuses attention on those areas which should receive priority consideration.

Generic avenues for solutions

99   A series of logical links have been determined to identify those avenues to solutions (A to M see below) which should be considered to address the factors raised by each question.

A   Rules and procedures - design

B   Rules and procedures - application

C   Training - rules and procedures

D   Training - hazards and risks

E   Safety commitment - workforce

F   safety commitment - management

G   Supervision - monitoring and detection

H   Supervision - style

I   Plant and equipment design and modification

J   Job design

K   Work conditions

L   Logistic support

M   Organisation

The matrix in the analysis charts (see Tables 5 to 8) presents those generic solution avenues (A to M) which are considered relevant to each of the 48 statements.

SELECTING APPROPRIATE SOLUTION AVENUES

100   The results from each of the three scoring methods must be entered, in turn, into this matrix in the highlighted boxes.

101   Tables 5 to 7 show the results for total scores, numbers of entries, and numbers of full mark scores being processed respectively. For each table, the scores in Columns A to M are simply added and noted at the foot of the table.

102   These three scores are then transferred into Table 8 which is used to select the suggested management strategy which is most appropriate to the given potential difficulties.

103   Although a purely mechanistic procedure may not be appropriate for all situations, the following guidelines are offered for selecting the generic solution routes which represent the best management strategy:

•   the assessor first identifies the top three total scores in Column A of Table 8 and marks them - in this example they are the 213, 205 and 204 scores representing solution avenues D, G and A respectively;

- the assessor then identifies the top three numbers of entries in Column B and marks them - these are the 68, 66 and 63 scores representing solution avenues A, D and G respecitively;

- the assessor identifies the top three 'full mark' six scores in Column C and marks them - these are the 14, 11 and 9 scores representing solution avenues G, D and I respectively.

Note: There are different numbers of entries possible under each generic solution avenue.

- Finally the assessor obtains a mean score by taking the total scores from Column A in Table 8 and dividing each by the number of potential entries in the matrix for each solution avenue. For example, as Solution A has 19 entries, the total score of 204 is divided by 19 to obtain the mean score of 10.7. Likewise the total score for Solution L is divided by 8 - the number of entries in the matrix under Column L - to give a mean score of 11.9.

- Using the number of column entries shown in Table 8, the mean scores are obtained and entered into Column D. Again the highest three are identified. These are the 14.4, 14.3 and 13.7 scores of K, I and G respectively.

Note: Additional selections can be made if the fourth rankings are close to the score for the third. For example, in Column C the third ranking is 9 and the fourth ranking is 8.

- Priority generic solutions are then selected where at least three scoring methods are marked.

- Secondary generic solutions are identified by one or two scoring methods being marked.

104   Each generic solution avenue is expanded to give a more complete set of suggestions for management to consider. As many problems will be specific to an industry, several of the solutions suggested will not be relevant or practical. It is the intention however that within each solution section there should be sufficient advice for management to be able to determine intervention strategies which are appropriate for their industry. In many instances it is not possible for these suggestions to be overly prescriptive as the most effective solution strategies are likely to be dependent on factors such as the specific plant, operations undertaken and local management and workforce issues.

105 At this stage, management can either address the important solution avenues which have been generated for a specific rule set which was studied or alternatively, can study the solution avenues for each rule set and determine the strategy which would best apply across all the rule sets being assessed. This latter approach would identify the potentially most powerful solution avenues for the organisation.

106 The management recommendations for each solution route are given in the section following the completed questionnaires and charts.

Table 2 Example of completed individual questionnaire

	Generic rule set	Score
1	The rules do not always describe the best way of working	0
2	Supervision recognises that deviations from rules are unavoidable	3
3	Schedules seldom allow enough time to do the job according to the rules	3
4	There are some rules which would make the job less safe/efficient	3
5	I sometimes can't get the equipment needed to work to the rules	0
6	Some rules are impossible or extremely difficult to apply	0
7	It is necessary to bend some rules to achieve a target	3
8	The rules are not written in simple language	0
9	Some rules are very difficult to understand	0
10	Rules commonly refer to other rules	0
11	Some rules are factually incorrect	0
12	I have found better ways of doing my job than those given in the rules	3
13	Sometimes the operating limits prescribed in rules are too restrictive	3
14	I often encounter situations where no prescribed actions are available	6
15	There are no general guidelines to use when specific rules do not apply	3
16	I sometimes don't know why I have to follow rules	0
17	Some rules do not need to be followed to get the job done safely	3
18	Some rules are only for inexperienced workers	0
19	Some rules are so complex that I lose track	0
20	Some rules are only of value to protect management's back	0
21	Sometimes conditions at the workplace stop me working to the rules	1
22	No system exists to check people understand procedures before they are used	0
23	Infringements of rules occur all the time	0
24	There are incentives to ignore some rules	0
25	I can get the job done quicker by ignoring some rules	3
26	Deviations from rules are not always corrected by a superior	3
27	Short cuts are acceptable when they involve little or no risk	3
28	There are circumstances where managers will support rules being broken	0
29	Management sometimes pressure people to break rules	0
30	The workforce sometimes pressure people to break rules	0
31	Staff shortages sometimes result in rules being broken to get the job done	1
32	There are some rules where your natural reaction would be to break them	3
33	Contractors are allowed different safety standards	3
34	There is no efficient procedure to monitor that rules are kept to	3
35	Supervisors seldom discipline workers who break rules	1
36	It is unlikely that somebody would be detected if they broke the rules	0
37	There are no personal benefits from strictly following rules and procedures	0
38	There are financial rewards to be gained from breaking the rules	6
39	I am sometimes tempted to do work that is not my responsibility	0
40	I am not given regular break periods when I do repetitive and boring jobs	0
41	Working to the rules removes skills	0
42	Deviating from some rules demonstrates knowledge of the job	0
43	I sometimes have difficulty getting hold of written rules and procedures	0
44	I sometimes come across a rule I did not know about	0
45	I have rules for tasks I will never have to do	0
46	I have not been trained in rules to be used in unusual circumstances	0
47	I often come across situations with which I am unfamiliar	3
48	I sometimes fail to fully understand which rules apply	0

disagree - 0   slightly agree - 1   agree - 3   strongly agree - 6

Table 3   Collation of individual questionnaire scores - 10 questionnaires

		Slightly agree x1	Agree x3	Strongly agree x6
Generic rule set				
1	The rules do not always describe the best way of working	0	4	2
2	Supervision recognises that deviations from rules are unavoidable	2	3	0
3	Schedules seldom allow enough time to do the job according to the rules	1	1	0
4	There are some rules which would make the job less safe/efficient	1	3	0
5	I sometimes can't get the equipment needed to work to the rules	0	1	3
6	Some rules are impossible or extremely difficult to apply	1	4	0
7	It is necessary to bend some rules to achieve a target	1	4	0
8	The rules are not written in simple language	0	0	0
9	Some rules are very difficult to understand	0	1	0
10	Rules commonly refer to other rules	4	2	0
11	Some rules are factually incorrect	1	2	0
12	I have found better ways of doing my job than those given in the rules	0	3	2
13	Sometimes the operating limits prescribed in rules are too restrictive	1	5	0
14	I often encounter situations where no prescribed actions are available	0	3	2
15	There are no general guidelines to use when specific rules do not apply	1	2	0
16	I sometimes don't know why I have to follow rules	0	1	0
17	Some rules do not need to be followed to get the job done safely	1	4	0
18	Some rules are only for inexperienced workers	0	4	0
19	Some rules are so complex that I lose track	0	1	0
20	Some rules are only of value to protect management's back	0	1	5
21	Sometimes conditions at the workplace stop me working to the rules	1	5	0
22	No system exists to check people understand procedures before they are used	0	1	2
23	Infringements of rules occur all the time	1	3	0
24	There are incentives to ignore some rules	1	1	0
25	I can get the job done quicker by ignoring some rules	0	4	2
26	Deviations from rules are not always corrected by a superior	0	2	2
27	Short cuts are acceptable when they involve little or no risk	0	4	0
28	There are circumstances where managers will support rules being broken	0	1	0
29	Management sometimes pressure people to break rules	1	1	0
30	The workforce sometimes pressure people to break rules	1	1	0
31	Staff shortages sometimes result in rules being broken to get the job done	0	4	2
32	There are some rules where your natural reaction would be to break them	1	4	0
33	Contractors are allowed different safety standards	1	3	0
34	There is no efficient procedure to monitor that rules are kept to	2	4	0
35	Supervisors seldom discipline workers who break rules	1	3	0
36	It is unlikely that somebody would be detected if they broke the rules	1	3	0
37	There are no personal benefits from strictly following rules and procedures	0	3	2
38	There are financial rewards to be gained from breaking the rules	1	1	0
39	I am sometimes tempted to do work that is not my responsibility	1	2	3
40	I am not given regular break periods when I do repetitive and boring jobs	0	1	0
41	Working to the rules removes skills	0	2	0
42	Deviating from some rules demonstrates knowledge of the job	1	1	0
43	I sometimes have difficulty getting hold of written rules and procedures	0	1	0
44	I sometimes come across a rule I did not know about	0	2	0
45	I have rules for tasks I will never have to do	1	1	0
46	I have not been trained in rules to be used in unusual circumstances	0	3	0
47	I often come across situations with which I am unfamiliar	0	2	0
48	I sometimes fail to fully understand which rules apply	1	1	0

Table 4   Analysis of questionnaire scores

Question number	A Total scores	B Number of entries	C Number of '6' marks
1	24	6	2
2	11	5	0
3	4	2	0
4	10	4	0
5	21	4	3
6	13	5	0
7	13	5	0
8	0	0	0
9	3	1	0
10	10	6	0
11	7	3	0
12	21	5	2
13	16	6	0
14	21	5	2
15	7	3	0
16	3	1	0
17	13	5	0
18	12	4	0
19	3	1	0
20	3	1	0
21	16	6	0
22	9	3	2
23	10	4	0
24	4	2	0
25	24	6	2
26	18	4	2
27	12	4	0
28	3	1	0
29	4	2	0
30	4	2	0
31	24	6	2
32	13	5	0
33	10	4	0
34	14	6	0
35	10	4	0
36	10	4	0
37	25	5	2
38	4	2	0
39	25	6	3
40	3	1	0
41	6	2	0
42	4	2	0
43	3	1	0
44	6	2	0
45	4	2	0
46	9	3	0
47	6	2	0
48	4	2	0

Table 5 The matrix analysis chart for total scores (from Column A)

Generic question set		Score	A	B	C	D	E	F	G	H	I	J	K	L	M
1	The rules do not always describe the best way of working	24	24	-	24	24	-	-	-	-	24	-	24	-	-
2	Supervision recognise that deviations from rules are unavoidable	11	11	-	-	-	-	11	-	11	11	-	11	-	-
3	Schedules seldom allow enough time to do the job according to the rules	4	4	-	-	-	-	4	-	-	4	-	-	4	-
4	There are some rules which would make the job less safe/efficient	10	10	-	-	-	10	-	-	-	10	-	10	-	-
5	I sometimes can't get the equipment needed to work to the rules	21	-	21	-	-	-	-	21	-	21	-	-	21	-
6	Some rules are impossible or extremely difficult to apply	13	-	13	-	-	-	-	-	-	13	13	13	-	-
7	It is necessary to bend some rules to achieve a target	13	-	-	13	13	13	13	-	-	-	-	-	-	-
8	The rules are not written in simple language	0	-	0	0	-	-	-	-	-	-	-	-	-	-
9	Some rules are very difficult to understand	3	3	3	3	-	-	-	-	-	-	-	-	-	-
10	Rules commonly refer to other rules	10	-	10	-	-	-	-	-	-	-	-	-	10	-
11	Some rules are factually incorrect	7	7	-	-	-	-	-	-	-	-	-	-	-	7
12	I have found better ways of doing my job than those given in the rules	21	21	-	-	21	-	-	-	-	21	21	-	-	-
13	Sometimes the operating limits prescribed in rules are too restrictive	16	16	-	-	16	-	-	-	-	-	16	-	-	-
14	I often encounter situations where no prescribed actions are available	21	21	-	-	-	-	-	-	-	-	-	-	21	21
15	There are no general guidelines to use when specific rules do not apply	7	7	-	7	7	-	-	-	7	-	-	-	-	7
16	I sometimes don't know why I have to follow rules	3	-	-	3	3	-	-	-	3	-	-	-	-	-
17	Some rules do not need to be followed to get the job done safely	13	13	-	-	13	-	-	-	-	-	-	-	-	-
18	Some rules are only for inexperienced workers	12	-	-	-	12	12	-	-	-	-	-	-	-	-
19	Some rules are so complex that I lose track	3	-	3	3	-	-	-	-	-	-	-	-	-	-
20	Some rules are only of value to protect management's back	3	3	-	-	-	-	3	-	-	-	-	-	-	3
21	Sometimes conditions at the workplace stop me working to the rules	16	-	-	-	-	-	16	16	-	16	-	16	-	-
22	No system exists to check people understand procedures before they are used	9	-	-	9	-	-	9	9	-	-	-	-	-	9
23	Infringements of rules occur all the time	10	-	-	-	10	10	10	10	10	-	-	-	-	-
24	There are incentives to ignore some rules	4	-	-	-	-	-	4	4	-	-	4	-	-	4
25	I can get the job done quicker by ignoring some rules	24	24	-	-	24	24	-	24	-	24	-	24	-	-
26	Deviations from rules are not always corrected by a superior	18	-	-	-	-	-	18	18	18	-	-	-	-	-
27	Short cuts are acceptable when they involve little or no risk	12	-	-	-	12	12	-	12	-	-	-	-	-	-
28	There are circumstances where managers will support rules being broken	3	3	-	-	-	-	3	-	-	-	-	-	-	-
29	Management sometimes pressure people to break rules	4	-	-	-	4	-	4	-	-	4	-	-	-	4
30	The workforce sometimes pressure people to break rules	4	-	-	-	4	4	-	4	-	-	-	-	-	4
31	Staff shortages sometimes result in rules being broken to get the job done	24	-	-	-	-	-	24	24	-	-	-	-	24	-
32	There are some rules where your natural reaction would be to break them	13	13	-	-	-	-	-	-	-	13	-	-	-	-
33	Contractors are allowed different safety standards	10	10	-	-	-	-	10	-	-	-	-	-	-	10
34	There is no efficient procedure to monitor that rules are kept to	14	-	-	-	-	-	14	14	-	-	-	-	-	14
35	Supervisors seldom discipline workers who break rules	10	-	-	-	-	-	10	10	10	-	-	-	-	-
36	It is unlikely that somebody would be detected if they broke the rules	10	-	-	-	-	10	10	10	-	10	10	-	-	-
37	There are no personal benefits from strictly following rules and procedures	21	-	-	-	21	-	-	-	21	-	21	-	-	21
38	There are financial rewards to be gained from breaking the rules	4	-	-	-	-	-	4	-	-	-	-	-	-	4
39	I am sometimes tempted to do work that is not my responsibility	25	-	-	-	25	-	-	25	-	-	25	-	-	-
40	I am not given regular break periods when I do repetitive and boring jobs	3	-	-	-	-	-	-	-	-	-	3	3	-	-
41	Working to the rules removes skills	6	6	-	-	-	-	-	-	-	-	6	-	-	-
42	Deviating from some rules demonstrates knowledge of the job	4	-	-	-	4	4	-	4	-	-	4	-	-	-
43	I sometimes have difficulty getting hold of written rules and procedures	3	-	-	-	-	-	3	-	3	-	-	3	-	-
44	I sometimes come across a rule I did not know about	6	-	-	6	-	-	-	-	-	-	-	-	6	-
45	I have rules for tasks I will never have to do	4	4	4	4	-	-	-	-	-	-	-	-	-	-
46	I have not been trained in rules to be used in unusual circumstances	9	-	9	9	-	-	-	-	-	-	-	-	-	-
47	I often come across situations with which I am unfamiliar	6	-	-	6	-	-	-	-	-	-	6	-	6	-
48	I sometimes fail to fully understand which rules apply	4	4	4	4	-	-	-	-	-	-	-	-	-	-
	Sum of total scores		204	67	91	213	99	170	205	83	171	129	101	95	108

29

Table 6   The matrix analysis chart - number of entries (Column B)

Generic question set		Score	A	B	C	D	E	F	G	H	I	J	K	L	M
1	The rules do not always describe the best way of working	6	6	-	-	6	6	-	-	-	6	-	6	-	-
2	Supervision recognise that deviations from rules are unavoidable	5	5	-	-	-	-	5	-	5	5	-	5	-	-
3	Schedules seldom allow enough time to do the job according to the rules	2	2	-	-	-	-	2	-	-	2	-	2	-	-
4	There are some rules which would make the job less safe/efficient	4	4	-	-	-	4	-	-	-	4	-	4	-	-
5	I sometimes can't get the equipment needed to work to the rules	4	-	4	-	-	-	-	4	-	4	-	-	4	-
6	Some rules are impossible or extremely difficult to apply	5	-	5	-	-	-	-	-	-	5	5	5	-	-
7	It is necessary to bend some rules to achieve a target	5	-	-	5	5	5	5	5	-	-	-	-	-	-
8	The rules are not written in simple language	0	-	0	0	-	-	-	-	-	-	-	-	-	-
9	Some rules are very difficult to understand	1	1	1	1	-	-	-	-	-	-	-	-	-	-
10	Rules commonly refer to other rules	6	-	6	-	-	-	-	-	-	-	-	-	6	-
11	Some rules are factually incorrect	3	3	-	-	-	-	-	-	-	-	-	-	-	3
12	I have found better ways of doing my job than those given in the rules	5	5	-	-	5	-	-	-	-	5	5	-	-	-
13	Sometimes the operating limits prescribed in rules are too restrictive	6	6	-	-	6	-	-	-	-	6	-	-	-	-
14	I often encounter situations where no prescribed actions are available	5	5	-	-	-	-	-	-	-	-	-	-	5	5
15	There are no general guidelines to use when specific rules do not apply	3	3	-	-	3	3	-	-	3	-	-	-	-	3
16	I sometimes don't know why I have to follow rules	1	-	-	1	1	-	-	-	1	-	-	-	-	-
17	Some rules do not need to be followed to get the job done safely	5	5	-	-	-	5	-	-	-	-	-	-	-	-
18	Some rules are only for inexperienced workers	4	-	-	-	4	4	-	-	-	-	-	-	-	-
19	Some rules are so complex that I lose track	1	-	1	1	-	-	-	-	-	-	-	-	-	-
20	Some rules are only of value to protect management's back	1	1	-	-	-	-	1	-	-	-	-	-	-	1
21	Sometimes conditions at the workplace stop me working to the rules	6	-	-	-	-	-	6	6	-	6	-	6	-	-
22	No system exists to check people understand procedures before they are used	3	-	-	3	-	-	3	3	-	-	-	-	-	3
23	Infringements of rules occur all the time	4	-	-	-	4	4	4	4	4	-	-	-	-	-
24	There are incentives to ignore some rules	2	-	-	-	-	-	2	2	-	-	2	-	-	2
25	I can get the job done quicker by ignoring some rules	6	6	-	-	6	6	-	6	-	6	-	6	-	-
26	Deviations from rules are not always corrected by a superior	4	-	-	-	-	-	4	4	4	-	-	-	-	-
27	Short cuts are acceptable when they involve little or no risk	4	-	-	-	4	4	-	4	-	-	-	-	-	-
28	There are circumstances where managers will support rules being broken	1	1	-	-	-	-	1	-	-	-	-	-	-	-
29	Management sometimes pressure people to break rules	2	-	-	-	2	-	2	-	-	2	-	-	-	2
30	The workforce sometimes pressure people to break rules	2	-	-	-	2	2	-	2	-	-	-	-	-	2
31	Staff shortages sometimes result in rules being broken to get the job done	6	-	-	-	-	-	6	6	-	-	-	6	-	-
32	There are some rules where your natural reaction would be to break them	5	5	-	-	-	-	-	-	-	5	-	-	-	-
33	Contractors are allowed different safety standards	4	4	-	-	-	-	4	-	-	-	-	-	-	4
34	There is no efficient procedure to monitor that rules are kept to	6	-	-	-	-	-	6	6	-	-	-	-	-	6
35	Supervisors seldom discipline workers who break rules	4	-	-	-	-	-	4	4	4	-	-	-	-	-
36	It is unlikely that somebody would be detected if they broke the rules	4	-	-	-	-	4	4	4	-	4	4	-	-	-
37	There are no personal benefits from strictly following rules and procedures	5	-	-	-	5	-	-	-	5	-	5	-	-	5
38	There are financial rewards to be gained from breaking the rules	2	-	-	-	-	-	2	-	-	-	-	-	-	2
39	I am sometimes tempted to do work that is not my responsibility	6	-	-	-	6	-	-	6	-	-	6	-	-	-
40	I am not given regular break periods when I do repetitive and boring jobs	1	-	-	-	-	-	-	-	-	1	1	-	-	-
41	Working to the rules removes skills	2	2	-	-	-	-	-	-	-	-	2	-	-	-
42	Deviating from some rules demonstrates knowledge of the job	2	-	-	-	2	2	-	2	-	-	2	-	-	-
43	I sometimes have difficulty getting hold of written rules and procedures	1	-	-	-	-	-	1	-	1	-	-	1	-	-
44	I sometimes come across a rule I did not know about	2	-	-	2	-	-	-	-	-	-	-	2	-	-
45	I have rules for tasks I will never have to do	2	2	2	2	-	-	-	-	-	-	-	-	-	-
46	I have not been trained in rules to be used in unusual circumstances	3	-	3	3	-	-	-	-	-	-	-	-	-	-
47	I often come across situations with which I am unfamiliar	2	-	-	2	-	-	-	-	-	-	2	-	2	-
48	I sometimes fail to fully understand which rules apply	2	2	2	2	-	-	-	-	-	-	-	-	-	-
	Sum of number of entries		66	24	31	64	35	62	63	27	54	40	33	28	38

Table 7   The matrix analysis chart - number of full mark scores (Column C)

Generic question set		Score	A	B	C	D	E	F	G	H	I	J	K	L	M
1	The rules do not always describe the best way of working	2	2	-		2	2	-	-	-	2	-	2	-	-
2	Supervision recognise that deviations from rules are unavoidable	0	0		-	-	-	-	0	-	0	0	-	0	-
3	Schedules seldom allow enough time to do the job according to the rules	0	0		-	-	-	-	0	-	0	-	-	0	-
4	There are some rules which would make the job less safe/efficient	0	0		-	-	-	0	-	-	0	-	0	-	-
5	I sometimes can't get the equipment needed to work to the rules	3	-	3	-	-	-	-	3	-	3	-	-	3	-
6	Some rules are impossible or extremely difficult to apply	0	-	0	-	-	-	-	-	-	0	0	0	-	-
7	It is necessary to bend some rules to achieve a target	0	-	-	0	0	0	0	0						
8	The rules are not written in simple language	0	-	0	0										
9	Some rules are very difficult to understand	0	0	0	0	0	-							-	
10	Rules commonly refer to other rules	0	-	0	-	-	-	-	-	-	-	-	-	0	-
11	Some rules are factually incorrect	0	0		-										0
12	I have found better ways of doing my job than those given in the rules	2	2	-	-	2	-	-	-		2	2	-	-	-
13	Sometimes the operating limits prescribed in rules are too restrictive	0	0	-	-	0	-	-	-	-	0	-	-	-	
14	I often encounter situations where no prescribed actions are available	2	2											2	2
15	There are no general guidelines to use when specific rules do not apply	0	0	-	0	0	-	-	-	0	-	-	-		0
16	I sometimes don't know why I have to follow rules	0	-	-	0	0	-	-	-	0	-				
17	Some rules do not need to be followed to get the job done safely	0	0	-	-	0	-	-	-	-	-	-	-		
18	Some rules are only for inexperienced workers	0	-	-	-	0	0	-							
19	Some rules are so complex that I lose track	0	-	0	0	-	-	-	-	-	-				
20	Some rules are only of value to protect management's back	0	0	-	-	-	-	0	-	-	-	-	-		0
21	Sometimes conditions at the workplace stop me working to the rules	0	-	-	-	-	-	0	0	-	0	-	0	-	
22	No system exists to check people understand procedures before they are used	2	-	-	2	-	-	2	2	-	-	-	-	-	2
23	Infringements of rules occur all the time	0	-	-	-	0	0	0	0	0	-	-	-	-	
24	There are incentives to ignore some rules	0	-	-	-	-	-	0	0	-	-	0	-	-	0
25	I can get the job done quicker by ignoring some rules	2	2	-	-	2	2	-	2	-	2	-	2	-	-
26	Deviations from rules are not always corrected by a superior	2	-	-	-	-	-	2	2	2	-	-	-	-	
27	Short cuts are acceptable when they involve little or no risk	0	-	-	-	0	0	-	0	-	-	-	-		
28	There are circumstances where managers will support rules being broken	0	0	-	-	-	-	0	-	-	-	-	-		
29	Management sometimes pressure people to break rules	0	-	-	-	0	-	0	-	-	0	-	-	-	0
30	The workforce sometimes pressure people to break rules	0	-	-	-	0	0	-	0	-	-	-	-	-	0
31	Staff shortages sometimes result in rules being broken to get the job done	2	-	-	-	-	-	2	2	-	-	-	-	2	-
32	There are some rules where your natural reaction would be to break them	0	0	-	-	-	-	-	-	-	0	-	-		
33	Contractors are allowed different safety standards	0	0	-	-	-	-	0	-	-	-	-	-	-	0
34	There is no efficient procedure to monitor that rules are kept to	0	-	-	-	-	-	0	0	-	-	-	-	-	0
35	Supervisors seldom discipline workers who break rules	0	-		-	-	-	0	0	0	-	-	-		
36	It is unlikely that somebody would be detected if they broke the rules	0	-	-	-	-	0	0	0	-	0	0	-		
37	There are no personal benefits from strictly following rules and procedures	2	-	-	-	2	-	-	2	-	2	-	2	-	2
38	There are financial rewards to be gained from breaking the rules	0	-	-	-	-	-	0	-	-	-	-	-	-	0
39	I am sometimes tempted to do work that is not my responsibility	3	-	-	-	3	-	-	3	-	-	3	-	-	-
40	I am not given regular break periods when I do repetitive and boring jobs	0	-	-	-	-	-	-	-	-	-	0	0	-	
41	Working to the rules removes skills	0	0	-	-	-	-	-	-	-	0	-	-		
42	Deviating from some rules demonstrates knowledge of the job	0	-	-	-	0	0	-	0	-	-	0	-	-	
43	I sometimes have difficulty getting hold of written rules and procedures	0	-	-	-	-	-	0	-	0	-	-	-	0	
44	I sometimes come across a rule I did not know about	0	-	-	0	-	-	-	-	-	-	-	-	0	
45	I have rules for tasks I will never have to do	0	0	0	0	-	-	-	-	-	0	-			
46	I have not been trained in rules to be used in unusual circumstances	0	-	0	0	-	-	-	-	-	-	-	-	-	
47	I often come across situations with which I am unfamiliar	0	-	-	0	-	-	-	-	-	0	-	0		
48	I sometimes fail to fully understand which rules apply	0	0	0	0	-	-	-	-	-	-	-			
	Sum of number of full mark scores		8	3	4	11	2	6	14	4	9	7	4	7	6

Table 8 Selection of solution avenues for given rule set

Generic avenues for solutions		A Total score	B Nos entries	C Nos '6'	D Mean score		Selection
A	Rules and procedures - aims and objectives	204*	68*	(8)	divide by 19	10.7	Secondary
B	Rules and procedures - application	67	24	3	divide by 9	7.4	
C	Training - rules and procedures	91	31	4	divide by 13	7.0	
D	Training - hazards and risks	213*	66*	11*	divide by 16	(13.3)	Priority
E	Safety commitment - workforce	99	35	2	divide by 19	11.0	
F	Safety commitment - management	170	(62)	6	divide by 18	9.4	
G	Supervision - monitoring and detection	205*	63*	14*	divide by 15	13.7*	Priority
H	Supervision - style	83	27	4	divide by 8	10.4	
I	Plant and equipment design and modification	171	54	9*	divide by 12	14.3*	Secondary
J	Job design	129	40	7	divide by 11	11.7	
K	Work conditions	101	33	4	divide by 7	14.4*	Secondary
L	Logistic support	95	28	7	divide by 8	11.9	
M	Organisation	108	38	6	divide by 12	9.0	

Use * to identify the top three scores in columns A-D. Priority generic solutions are selected where at least three scoring methods are marked *.

RECOMMENDATIONS FOR SOLUTIONS

107   This section gives an overview of guidelines, hints and suggestions under each of the general solution avenues (A to M) which are used in the main analysis. These should be used in conjunction with the results of the relevant interview questions (see 'Methodology' and Appendix 3) and, where applicable, the results of individual answers to the main question set.

108   These can never be totally relevant to every situation, as factors specific to each plant, or method of operation, will make some of the ideas unworkable or inapplicable.

109   For each of the following action routes, ideas should be selected which ideally remove the problem at source. Only if this ideal cannot be achieved should actions be considered which reduce the probability of the incident occurring. In such circumstances, it is also important to address ways of reducing the severity of the incident as the incident may still occur, albeit at a reduced probability.

A   Rules and procedures: correct aims and objectives

110   Rules should be practical and easily understood by those who will use them. This section summarises factors to consider when developing rules and procedures to ensure they are sound and compatible with the range of operations undertaken.

111   A badly thought through rule may, in some cases, prove impractical or impossible to apply in certain circumstances. One rule may contradict another rule. Rules may be over-restrictive in some situations. On the other hand, rules may be so general that they offer no genuine help and may be so vague that it could always be argued that they were complied with - even following an accident. Rules and procedures which are considered unnecessary are just a burden.

112   All of these problems have been identified in a range of large organisations. Very often, rules are not thought through properly - often as a hasty response to an incident. It could even be argued that some were produced simply with the intention of protecting management's position in the event of another accident.

113   As a result of certain badly considered rules, some violations may be necessary to perform the job. Rules are sometimes broken in an attempt to counteract over-restriction, in a genuine attempt to help the organisation meet its performance goals.

114   It is therefore vital that rules are reviewed to ensure their relevance and practicality before trying to ensure compliance with them. Management should rigorously check all procedures to ensure that none are incompatible, and periodically check them especially when new procedures have been introduced.

115   It is valuable to bear these aspects in mind when formulating new rules. A technically perfect rule should:

- have a clear and acceptable aim;

- as far as possible, represent the best and most efficient way of doing the job safely. Rules which require excessive time and energy will be violated;

- be clearly and precisely expressed, leaving no loopholes or room for doubt about its application in any particular situation;

- be certain to achieve the purpose, without undesirable side effects;

- be limited in number if the employee is supposed to remember them all. Otherwise, procedures should be easily accessible and time should be allowed within the task to refer to them;

- be initially assessed by members of the workforce and management to ensure they are (a) practical, (b) easy to follow, and (c) fully understood by the workforce.

B   Rules and procedures: correct application and presentation

116   A good rule can fail if it is badly presented to the workforce. The basic requirements of the rule can be written in such a convoluted way that they are incomprehensible to many members of the workforce. In some situations the rules are not well presented and vital information is hidden in complex and occasionally legal jargon. Rules can be written in an attempt by writers to show off their knowledge, rather than their ability to effectively express the vital points contained in them.

117   Incidents have been identified in the mining industry where employees have not even looked at the Manager's Rules, presumably because of the daunting nature of their presentation.

118   This section summarises the factors you need to consider when deciding how to present and apply the rulings you have identified as appropriate.

- Where rules and procedures are more relevant to some situations than others, a degree of flexibility should be written in.

- The applicability and accuracy of rules and procedures can often be improved by involving users in writing them. A spin-off of this approach is that it will increase the sense of ownership by the workforce, who will be more likely to comply with rules they have helped to write.

- A rule which was entirely appropriate and correct at the time of writing may gradually lose relevance as methods and workstation designs evolve. It is therefore desirable to put in place a system of feedback so staff can update procedures and make any necessary changes.

- A good rule can soon become impractical if the equipment/facilities required to keep it are not readily available. It is therefore important to ensure that if certain equipment is required to carry out a procedure, it is available and properly maintained.

- The wording and style of rules and procedures should be easy to understand. Keep sentences short and long words to a minimum. Direct language is clearer than indirect, eg 'Read dial A and write it in the logbook' is better than 'A reading of the output shown on dial A should be taken and a recording made in the logbook'.

- Rules and procedures should be indexed so they can be referred to easily.

- If an instruction is difficult to explain verbally, an illustration might help.

119   Finally, management should check, as part of a commissioning exercise, that every member of the workforce has a good working knowledge and accepts all safety procedures.

C   Training: rules and procedures

120   Good training is often assumed - simply because training is a formal requirement for those employed in an industry. There are, however, many assumptions which are made about the quality of the safety training provided. The two most common assumptions are:

(a)   that the training addresses all the relevant safety issues; and

(b)   that the training was initially effective and will continue to be effective.

121   Central to both potential problem areas is a lack of measurement of training effectiveness, both immediately after the training and periodically (eg annually) after the training. The latter can be important to determine a need for any specific refresher training. Measures for testing understanding may therefore need to be developed and applied.

Measuring the effectiveness of training

122   Without this measurement of training effectiveness there can be no systematic feedback to the trainers to show where elements of the training packages could be improved to better convey the information on the rules or where selected individuals may require further tuition. If, for example, the feedback shows that about 60% of the trainees have not fully understood certain issues on the course, then it would suggest that the training course/material would benefit from being reviewed. In such an event, the implications would be that most of the workforce could have a serious lack of understanding, which under certain circumstances could lead to errors and subsequent accidents/incidents.

123   If, on the other hand, the feedback shows that only 10% of trainees are having difficulty, then clearly the training course is effective for the vast majority of trainees and would probably not need further consideration. In this case the feedback suggests that there are a small number of trainees with special difficulties who have additional training needs.

124   Care should be taken when using the test results of many training courses. Especially with some of the computer learning packages, the final tests can simply be a measure of a trainee's short-term memory and not of a deeper understanding of the important factors relevant to safety. For example a test may simply ask a trainee to restate the order of operations in a complex task. A deeper understanding of the safety issues may better be tested by targeting the trainee's understanding of the consequences of not adhering to the various operation stage rules.

Refresher training needs

125   Many industries have policies to repeat facets of safety training at fixed intervals. In practice, the need for retraining and the period between training sessions are often decided by management on the grounds of best judgement and practicality. Although in many circumstances the retraining arrangements may be satisfactory, there are likely to be instances where a more systematic approach would prove beneficial.

126   A wide range of factors will determine the individual's need for refresher training. For example a person will probably need more refresher training on a task rarely performed than on one regularly performed. A change in work methods or equipment specification may also suggest retraining.

127   The specific needs of each operator may be determined by supervisors regularly asking them to demonstrate their skills and understanding of procedures etc.

D   Training: hazard awareness and risk perception

128   Behaviour is strongly influenced by a persons awareness of hazards in the workplace. With little or no awareness people will more readily deviate from the rules and procedures of the workplace. Indeed, these rules are likely to be seen more as simple restrictions on actions rather than good and safe working practices. For example when working with trichloroethane, workers may ignore a no smoking rule because they find that the chemical is not easily set alight. In fact, the rule exists because the hot cigarette-end breaks the vapour down into toxic gases, which the smoker then inhales.

129   Once an individual is aware of the existence of the hazard, the next important question is how much risk does the individual associate with deviations from the prescribed rules and procedures. Underestimation of risks may be common. Many older workers, for example, appear to think that there is little risk to their hearing from working in noisy environments. Some of these people are therefore very reluctant to comply with local requirements to wear hearing protection. Similar problems are sometimes found with eye protection.

130   The assessment of hazard awareness and risk perceptions is therefore central to an understanding of the reasons behind some rule violations. There is, however, a further dimension to consider. The decision to commit a violation is often derived from a conscious decision which balances the perceived risks against the perceived benefits.

131   Thus, when assessing the training needs associated with reducing rule violations it is important to obtain some understanding of:

•   the degree to which the workforce understands the hazards;

•   the risk they will incur if they choose to deviate from each rule;

•   the benefits (both to themselves and their organisation) which they perceive would come from breaking each rule.

132   The benefits may be short term or long term. They may be personal benefits (eg ego needs, financial rewards, compliance with group norms) as well as benefits for the company (eg more production, faster repairs).

133   It is likely that the exact balance of risks and benefits will differ throughout the workforce so any single management approach will be more effective for some of the workforce than for others. As a result, management can never be sure that their actions will be satisfactory for all their staff. They may be confident that their actions have moved attitudes in the right direction, but they can never be certain that they have gone far enough, for all the workforce.

134   It is important to measure changes in attitudes throughout any programme of change. The data collected should be sufficient to allow management to focus on those rules and procedures requiring further attention and those aspects of risk/benefits which need to be addressed.

135   Questionnaires have been successfully used. The main problem, however, is the initial identification of the detailed behavioural factors which need to be measured. For example the assessment will probably need to address specific risk areas such as, anchoring a fall-arrest harness system to a handrail (which is not designed or tested to safely take the high g-force loading which can occur during an arrest), as opposed to anchoring a fall-arrest harness system to an approved fixture. A small multi-disciplinary team, consisting of representatives of the workforce, safety and training departments, should be able to quickly identify the unsafe behaviour that should be examined first.

136   These detailed scenarios can never fully represent all the risk factors, and in practice they probably do not need to. Actions taken to heighten people's perceptions of risks in several areas may produce additional benefits of better risk perceptions in general. The exposure of the factors (previously not considered) which could combine to create the tangible safety risk may be relevant to other areas which are not specifically addressed. The crucial point is to determine and assess a workable selection of critical behavioural situations. Less critical behaviour can then be targeted in subsequent assessments if necessary.

137   In particular, management should:

- develop a thorough understanding of the need for procedures (via accident case studies, potential accidents etc), and the consequences (safety and plant damage/lost production) resulting from failure to comply;

- clearly demonstrate the dangers of operating machinery and processes beyond the limits laid out in any safety or work procedures;

- provide a general safety knowledge of the whole system as well as detailed knowledge of all relevant specific plant;

- increase perception of risk by a variety of methods including interviews with actual victims. Risk communications should include consequences of accidents in terms of financial loss, effect on family, career and permanent disability;

- ensure that workers and supervisors are continually made aware of accidents and their costs;

- ensure that people are made aware of the likelihood of detection and disciplinary actions which would be taken against them. It is important, however, that this should not detract from a 'no blame - near miss' reporting culture which can be very effective for addressing inadvertent breaking of rules.

E   Safety commitment: the workforce

138   A problem frequently experienced is that the good working practices and attitudes of a well-trained new recruit will be lost when he or she returns to the workplace alongside experienced workers. Bad habits will tend to be transferred to the new recruit, rather than good habits being transferred to the experienced workers. Without measures to improve the general attitudes of the workforce, many safety initiatives may fail, or at least be less effective than was hoped.

139   Invariably, a large proportion of the safety commitment of the workforce stems from the perceived safety commitment of senior staff - see Section F. Nevertheless there are other influences to address.

140   Some organisations appear to have achieved success by a number of initiatives in this area.

- Involving the workforce in serious campaigns to improve measurable safety parameters - perhaps with token prizes/rewards for sustained safety performances which can create a sort of competition between teams to improve safety standards. This may be difficult to manage initially, however it is likely to be successful if management can introduce initiatives to create, and maintain, a strong pride among the workforce in the adoption of good safety standards.

- Management should provide an effective reporting procedure for workers to use in cases where they consider they are being pressured by other members of the workforce. This should then be drawn to the attention of appropriate supervisors to prevent any recurrence.

- Involving the workforce in the drafting of safety rules is a good way of promoting good compliance with safety rules. It encourages a feeling of ownership of those rules and procedures and has proved successful in a number of organisations.

- Training the workforce on the basic safety rules associated with all jobs will both widen their perceptions of safety matters and also better expose employees who break safety rules and procedures. For example an electrician working with production workers could break some rules without the rest of the workforce being aware of it. If the workforce understood the need for electricians to safely isolate equipment (both for their own safety and the safety of those working nearby), they would be more likely to put pressure on the electricians to work safely.

F   Safety commitment: management

141   Management are quick to claim the right to decide how they will ensure profit and the future of the company. They should be equally willing to decide how they will pursue the safety goals. They should not merely require safety, leaving it up to the employees to decide how to reach that goal. Repeated studies, both in UK mining and other industries, have demonstrated the pivotal effect which the safety commitment of management has on the attitudes and subsequent behaviour of those operating below them in the organisation.

142   The vital point is that it is no good managers being personally committed to safety if this is not conveyed to the workforce in their actions. Questionnaires completed by the workforce regularly imply that some management are less committed to safety than the managers themselves expected.

143   There are a number of explanations. Senior staff can easily walk past an operation where some of the safety procedures are not being followed, simply because they are preoccupied with an urgent problem elsewhere on site. Unfortunately, those involved in the violation may see this as proof that the senior member of staff condoned the unsafe activities and must have a lower commitment to safety than they previously assumed. Another common example is when senior management pass a noise zone without putting on ear defenders. Back at the safety meeting these managers may then criticise the staff for not complying with the rule on wearing of ear defenders in noise zones.

144   Managers may only show concern over efficiency and profit. Taken in isolation, these management priorities may create pressure (real or perceived) to violate, or at least to cut corners.

145   In order to demonstrate commitment to safety, management can:

- take into consideration an individual's safety record when making promotions;

- give regular and public praise to teams/individuals with good safety records/behaviour;

- create accountability procedures which make line management responsible for all safety costs in their district/department, including accident costs (lost time, compensation etc), and plant damage;

- if appropriate, investigate violations without (or separate from) any attribution of blame: any predisposing factors should then be highlighted and reduced as far as possible;

- as well as investigating accidents causing injury, address also any potential errors or near misses which have been reported by the workforce;

- devote more time to increase the visibility of efforts directed at safety;

- continually lead by example in safety matters and continually communicate their belief in safety;

- provide an effective reporting procedure (probably anonymous) for the workforce to use if they consider themselves pressured by supervisors to violate safety procedures - this would need to be seen to work effectively if it is to gain the trust of the workforce.

G   Supervision: monitoring and detection

146   A strong disincentive to rule violation is a high probability of detection (and subsequent disciplinary action). Thus, it is surprising that many work situations have poor supervision. There are a number of factors to consider in any programme which is designed to improve the chances of detecting rule violations. These factors cover both real-time monitoring and the ability to detect violations after the work has been completed.

147   *Real-time monitoring*

- Especially where a supervisor has to cover a wide area, the predictability of times of inspection by supervision can allow correct methods to be adopted when an inspection is expected. Random checks by other functions, such as safety/training/management will help off-set this problem.

- Supervisors may not be fully trained on certain specialist working practices (eg high voltage working practices of electricians, or aspects of fork lift truck driving) and therefore may not be aware of deviations in approved working methods.

- Over time, the judgement of a supervisor may drift to overestimating or underestimating safety risk associated with a particular operation. It is desirable to monitor the judgement of supervisors, with refresher training given where necessary.

- Many safety assessments concentrate on unsafe conditions, not unsafe behaviour.

- In a cost-conscious environment there may be strong pressures to improve productivity. In such conditions, some supervisors may not report every safety violation. Independent checks which identify safety issues not previously reported may reveal a need to re-emphasise the important role of the safety inspections.

148   *Post-task monitoring*

It is sometimes possible for a supervisor to check that the approved working methods have been adopted after completion of the work.

- Documentation should be designed to prevent/minimise misuse.

- Equipment can be designed to highlight where poor practices are taking place. For example colour coding all lifting equipment which has been tested and approved for use over a certain period will readily highlight situations where improvised methods are being adopted.

149   *Peer pressure*

Probably the most effective supervisors are the workforce themselves. Some industries have managed the attitudes of the workforce so that they will expect other workers to work strictly to the safety rules. Concern over their own safety, and pride in the quality of their work can often create an environment where a member of the workforce would be made to feel very uncomfortable if he or she deliberately chose to break safety rules.

H   Supervision: style

150   The quality and effectiveness of supervisors' style is a major influence on the probability of rule violations in areas under their control. Studies in UK mining and elsewhere have

consistently shown a link between the observable safety commitment of supervisors and the safety attitudes of the workforce reporting to them. This is to be expected. Employees are less likely to slow the job down by the strict adoption of safety rules if they do not believe their supervisors are fully committed to safety. To gain praise from their supervisors, the workers will adopt a working style which they think best matches their expectations. Supervisors should therefore understand that certain behaviour may be interpreted by the workforce as demonstrating a low commitment to safety which could encourage the workforce to adopt similar values.

151   Supervisors should also be effective in how they communicate safety methods and they should be fair and be seen to be fair in how they discipline workers who break safety rules. Supervisors should always stop poor work when they see it and always discipline (including verbal warnings) all those involved in any unsafe activity. Management should ensure that supervisors rigorously apply the agreed disciplinary procedures, for every disciplinary offence, or review the procedure if this approach is not always appropriate. Failure to do this can easily create the impression in the workforce that the supervisors are not serious about safety and that favouritism exists, where certain people are allowed 'to get away with it' when others are always punished.

152   Staff management skills concerned with motivating the workforce are very important. It is for example, often useful for the supervisor to 'attack' the bad practice and not the person when dealing with violations.

I   Plant and equipment design and modification

153   Today's designers have a duty under the Health and Safety at Work etc Act 1974 to design plant and equipment that is safe. If necessary, research should be carried out to ensure this. Where misuse can be forseen this should be taken into account and the design modified to encourage safe use.

154   A prime motive for employees to commit violations is that it makes their job easier. Central to this notion is the adequacy of the design of equipment. There is a wide range of poor design features which contribute to difficulty in operating a machine. These poor design features can, however, often be predicted as providing a strong motive for operators to violate some safety rules.

155   A good example was found on some of the underground locomotives which were used in the coal industry. Access to some cabs was extremely difficult due to the small hatch aperture, the step height into the cab and the poor design of hand and foot holds. When faced with a

need to enter and leave the cab over 100 times a shift, several drivers were tempted to violate a safety rule and drive the locomotive short distances (for example to couple and uncouple wagons) by leaning into the cabs. Unfortunately this led to serious and fatal accidents. Notices and training campaigns were not successful. These bad practices only disappeared when the locomotives themselves were improved to make access so easy that it was more difficult to drive the locomotive from outside the cab than from inside.

156   The following factors increase the probability of violations in deep mining. Many will apply equally to a wide range of industries.

• Controls which are excessively time consuming, physically tiring or awkward to operate.

• Working postures which are awkward or uncomfortable - physical pain or discomfort is a good motive for cutting corners or breaking rules if this either reduces the amount of pain or discomfort, or reduces the time an operator will be exposed to such problems.

• Difficulty in getting into and out of the operating position.

• Poor vision from the driving/operating position.

• Equipment which appears needlessly slow and which may cause people to improvise via other methods/equipment.

• Excessive machine speed capability: speed settings which are above the maximum permitted should be blanked off where the use of the excessive speed would not be reliably detected. Management should also ensure that an effective monitoring and control package is operational.

• Environmental problems of dust and fumes or exhaust building up at the operator location.

• Noise levels that interfere with communications or are annoying - some signals quickly become simply background noise and are damaged to put them out of use.

• Design features often prevent violations becoming visible to others (eg supervisors). Equipment can often be designed, or modified, to make it visually clear to the user and supervisors if it is being used in an inappropriate situation. A simple example would be the colour coding of lifting equipment which is tested and within its approval period.

157   Other problematic design factors include:

- uncomfortable, or difficult to use, personal protective equipment;

- instrumentation which is, or has been, unreliable and may be subsequently intentionally disregarded;

- alarm systems which give frequent false alarms, or which hide critical alarm messages within a large number of 'information only' alarms. The latter may cause operators to genuinely miss critical alarms, but such poor alarm system design may also result in operators deliberately ignoring screens full of alarm messages or accepting many without the full investigation required;

- static warnings which are always present, even when the danger is only intermittent, soon lose their effect. This can result in habitual, apparently trivial, violations that occasionally have serious consequences;

- similarly, general warnings that usually indicate a minor problem but more rarely a serious problem can cause people to misjudge the seriousness and habitually violate the warning.

158   In order to minimise the consequences of errors or violations, designers should, wherever possible, design systems which give operators clear warnings of violations and sufficient opportunity to recover from any error.

J   Job design

159   Jobs which have been designed or developed from theoretical optimum production methods are often very narrow and boring. As a result motivation to perform well is often reduced. Safety standards can drift as people experiment with alternative methods, either to increase performance or to prove to themselves they need not work in such a constrained environment.

160   There are many examples where companies have expanded the scope of jobs, either to provide a wider range of skills, or preferably to give employees the added depth of more responsibilities. It is however important to realise that many individuals will, at least initially, resent being given added tasks or responsibilities. Although many will eventually come to accept and enjoy the benefits these enlarged jobs bring, some may never accept changes to their jobs. To be successful, a company should ensure that any changes are sufficiently flexible to

allow those seeking new skills and responsibilities to flourish while those content with their current jobs are not seen to be lesser people if they do not take up these new challenges (or burdens).

161 There are a number of measurement procedures which can be used to determine the nature of any gross deficiencies in the design of jobs, especially regarding factors which adversely influence job satisfaction. The Job Diagnostic Survey (JDS) is one of many procedures which is relatively simple to apply. Full details of the JDS are given in Hackman and Oldham (1980).

162 Where there are problems, there are three main kinds of job design improvement to consider.

- Flexible working groups with collective responsibility for production and quality. Increased individual responsibility due to peer pressure and responsibility to the group. Workers see themselves as more important in a small group and an individual can have a big impact. Feedback of individual performance is much more likely and immediate. The work gives more satisfaction and people see themselves as performing a useful job.

- Job enlargement. The division of labour is reduced so that cycle times are increased, each person doing more than one task which can add up to a more satisfying job. This can develop broader skills, the use of discretion, feedback of results, and incorporate in a job the inter-related tasks which are associated with other products and services.

- Job enrichment. Unlike job enlargement, where 'more of the same' tends to be added to increase variety, job enrichment improves the challenging aspects of a job. A clerical worker might be made responsible for some management issues. Manual workers might be made responsible for managing their quality procedures and/or maintenance.

163 These job design methods are well described in the literature (Bailey, 1983).

164 It is important following any job design activity that management ensure that staff have the skills, knowledge and experience appropriate for the requirements of the new position.

K   Working conditions

165 Poor working conditions can cause errors and violations. Some important factors which need to be considered are noise, poor lighting, thermal environment, personal protective equipment (PPE).

Noise

166   It is well known that high noise levels are a health risk, but other aspects can create difficulties or annoyances for the workforce. Excessive noise levels or noise levels which are too quiet can also increase the likelihood of errors as a result of difficulties in concentration or low arousal levels. Noise can also interfere with speech and the ability to hear warning signals. This can be especially critical where reliable verbal communications are necessary for the safety of the workforce, or where a misunderstanding could lead to errors with safety implications. A useful technique for assessing and overcoming problems of signal audibility under such conditions is described in Simpson GC and Coleman GJ (1988).

Poor lighting

167   Selecting satisfactory lighting for a given workplace involves balancing several factors. However, for most practical purposes, suitable light levels can be found in ergonomic/lighting handbooks (CIBSE, 1989). You may need to consider individual attributes of workers, such as age. Where the workforce consists of predominantly older people, higher light levels may be justified.

168   Whatever the light levels selected, it is important that the design of the lighting eliminates, wherever possible, any glare. Glare is a common cause of eye strain and headaches and also reduces visual efficiency. In most workplaces daylight provides the most illumination. The enormous variations in daylight between overcast winter days and bright summer days, as well as the changes in direction of the light from morning to evening, present a challenge to the designers of some workstations.

Thermal environment

169   There are no absolute thermal limits which are suitable for all people all the time. In general, cooler conditions are required where physical work is undertaken than for sedentary jobs. Air movement is important. For sedentary jobs, a lower air movement is required than for physical jobs. Office workers, for example, frequently complain of draughts where the same air movement would be considered 'stuffy' for a workforce engaged in physical tasks. Clothing, in part, dictates suitability of the thermal conditions, with those choosing to wear light clothing requiring higher temperatures than those wearing jumpers and jackets.

170   Although management frequently provide PPE to the workforce, in many instances there is a reluctance to use it. For example people working in a noisy environment may decide not to wear any hearing protection. The reasons can be effectively summarised as (a) a failure to fully appreciate the risks involved, (b) features of the PPE make using it uncomfortable, irritating and adversely affecting the speed at which the job can be done, and (c) people think using the PPE actually creates other safety risks, eg they fear that they will not be able to hear any warning signals.

L   Logistic support

171   Many rules and procedures specify the use of certain equipment or the need for a certain number of people to be present before the operation should begin. Some operations require supporting information to be quickly available (eg either at the work site or readily obtained over the telephone) in the event of unforeseen circumstances arising.

172   All such requirements demand appropriate logistic support by the organisation. Difficulties often arise because, in practice, what should be freely available is in fact very difficult to obtain. Short cuts and other violations often result.

173   Management often assume that such support is available because it was originally specified or because it was available when the plant/equipment was commissioned. Often the problem is that missing logistic support can go unnoticed by senior management, and as a result alternative/improvised methods tend to be adopted. Once highlighted, however, management can usually easily ensure that the necessary support is returned and monitoring systems introduced to ensure the support remains readily available to the workforce.

174   The following logistic support deficiencies were identified in a number of studies conducted in a range of industries. Management should review their logistic support to ensure that these and other problems could not occur.

- The renewal of protective equipment is discontinued on the grounds that it is being abused, eg used away from work. Such abuse, of course, requires other management actions and not the removal of this important safety provision.

- Similarly, certain special tools are often not available to the workforce from the stores on the grounds that too many go missing. Because of difficulties maintenance crews usually experience in getting such tools, many resort to hiding them so they will at least be available to them when they need them. Poor security and management are no excuse for deliberately restricting the availability of tools needed to perform jobs safely.

- Occasions have been found where suitable fall arrest equipment was not available for the smaller and larger members of the workforce. The range of harnesses used did not cater for extremes in body sizes and no alternative was available.

- Technical documentation may not be available when new equipment is delivered. Where it is, it may be kept centrally (eg in the chief engineer's office) and not be readily available for routine use by maintenance crews.

- Prescribed operating methods may state a certain minimum staffing level (eg the presence of two people when transferring materials using powered lifting facilities, or the need to have a person at the top of a bunker when employees are working inside). There have been times when, perhaps due to deployment difficulties or emergency situations, such activities have been performed without the minimum staffing level.

- Many construction operations require the routine delivery of supplies. When the infrastructure fails to keep up deliveries of such supplies, improvised methods may be adopted.

M   Rationalise the work organisation

175   Senior management style, attitudes, policies, and the wider safety culture of an organisation can work directly, or indirectly, to increase the likelihood of violations. Where organisational solutions have been indicated, consider the following factors.

- Accident and reporting systems should avoid blaming individuals and recording remedial actions such as 'take more care in future'. Apportioning blame may be unhelpful because it puts the victim in a position of resistance and resentment. What is more important, it fails to take account of the influence of the management system on individual behaviour. When an injury results from a violation, the unsafe act has probably taken place many times before. Therefore, responsibility lies with the management system, not just the employee. The examination of underlying causes allows the company to learn from their experience and apply strategies which will reduce the likelihood of the same incident occurring again. At the same time, writing new procedures in response to every accident is unhelpful. The effect of tightening up procedures without considering their practicality in the real work situation can be to increase the likelihood of violations.

- When violations of rules have extremely serious consequences, alternatives to rules should be considered, eg defences.

- Rules which are written merely as defences against litigation are seen as such by staff and therefore should be avoided.

- Payment incentive schemes based purely on production should be avoided if they encourage violations. When there are production incentives, safety features may be overridden and implicit understandings between supervisors and workers may allow circumvention of safe practices. Formal, or informal, systems should not exist which effectively punish individuals who cost the company money by complying with rules.

- Schemes should be introduced to positively reward individuals who comply with the rules. It is more effective to reward compliance than to punish violations of rules. People's behaviour will change to avoid punishment only while the punishment continues, whereas reward can change behaviour permanently. Fines for speeding do not teach safe driving, they teach drivers to watch out for police cars. Management effort should therefore be devoted to creating an organisation which provides positive rewards for safe behaviour rather than focusing on the negative consequences following violations. Safe working can be rewarded simply through encouragement and other incentives, such as promotion opportunities.

- Compliance with safety rules should not cost employees money. Workers and managers alike may develop a belief that adherence to all safety rules would reduce production. Consequently, there may be compliance with only those rules that do not appear to cost time.

- Incentives should exist for individuals to reveal potential or actual violations. Confidential or anonymous reporting schemes may be appropriate. Employees should be encouraged to draw attention to weaknesses in rules or any factors which could result in temptations to violate.

- Financial accountability for accident costs should not be borne centrally, ie away from the source of many of the causes and line management functions responsible. Management should be held accountable for the full costs of accidents and downtimes through human error and violations. Supervisors should also be accountable for safety as well as production targets.

- The roles and responsibility for safety matters should be assessed to ensure there are no ambiguities, especially at senior levels. Management should identify and quickly clarify any ambiguities in roles and responsibilities which the workforce or supervision possess. It is the allocation of tasks for unusual circumstances and peripheral activities which often present the most problems.

- When discipline is required to enforce compliance, it should be consistent and fair, otherwise it can have negative effects. Management responsibilities for disciplining different working groups, and the different penalties for different offences, should be clear. Disciplinary actions should be agreed by the workforce as appropriate for each offence.

- Management should create an effective communication channel to them from the workforce to identify potential safety hazards, eg a no blame report facility/near miss reporting etc. The safety committee should not be the only forum for the discussion of safety issues. Management should ensure that there is effective communication between the various supervisory and worker levels and that there are a variety of informal modes of communication.

- There should be regular audits to identify, and remove, any rules which may have become obsolete over time by technical advances.

176　The exact effects of many of these factors can be difficult to accurately predict, however these wider organisational factors can be extremely influential in the safety performance of the company. Periodic reviews of all procedures and monitoring systems should therefore be introduced which are conducted by teams of management and the workforce.

APPENDIX 1   BIBLIOGRAPHY

Baily J (1983) *Job design and work organisation* Prentice Hall International

CIBSE (1989) *The industrial environment* LG1, The Chartered Institute of Building Services Engineers, London

Coleman et al (1984) *Communications in noisy environments* Final Report on CEC Contract 7206/00/8/09, Institute of Occupational Medicine, Edinburgh

Department of Transport (1988) *Investigation into the Clapham Junction railway accident* London, HMSO

Free R (1994) *Role of procedural violations in railway accidents* PhD Thesis Dept of Psychology University of Manchester (unpublished)

Hackman JR, Oldham GR (1980) *Work redesign* Addison-Wesley Publishing

Harper JG (1991) Traffic violation detection and deterrence: Implications for automatic policing *Applied Ergonomics* 1992,22.3,189-197

HFRG (1991) *Guide to reducing human error in process operations* SRD, UKAEA

HSC (1993) ACSNI Human Factors Study Group, Third Report: *Organising for Safety* HSE Books ISBN 0 7176 0865 4

HSE (1991) *Successful health and safety management* HS(G) 65 HSE Books ISBN 0 7176 0425 X

Krause R, Hidley JH, Lareau W (1984) Behavioural science applied to accident prevention *Professional Safety* Official publication of the American Society of Safety Engineers

Krause TR, Hidley JH, Hodson SJ (1990) *The behaviour-based safety process - managing involvement for an injury-free culture* Van Nostrand Reinhold, New York

Krause TR, Hidley JH, (1992) On their best behavior *Accident Prevention* June 1992, 11-14

Leather PJ (1987) Safety and accidents in the construction industry: A work design perspective *Work and Stress* 1987 1 No 2 167-174

Mason S (1992) Practical guidelines for improving safety through the reduction of human error *The Safety and Health Practitioner* May 1992

Mason S, Rushworth A M (1992) Human aspects of maintenance *Maintenance* 7 No 3

Meister D (1992) Some comments on the future of ergonomics *International Journal of Industrial Ergonomics* 257-260

Munipov VM (1992) Chernobyl operators: criminals or victims? *Applied Ergonomics* 23(5), 337-342

Rasmussen J (1987) The definition of human error and a taxonomy for technical system design. In Rasmussen, Duncan, Leplat (eds) *New technology and human error* Chichester, John Wiley and Sons

Reason J T (1990) *Human error* New York, Cambridge University Press

Rimington J (1993) Does health and safety at work pay? *Safety Management* September 1993

Rushworth A M, Best C F, Coleman G J, Graveling R A, Mason S, Simpson G C (1986) *Study of ergonomics principles in accident prevention for bunkers* Institute of Occupational Medicine, Final Report on CEC Contract 7247/12/049

Simpson G C and Coleman G J (1988) The development of a procedure to ensure effective warning signals *The Mining Engineer* May, 511 - 514

Smith E J, Harris M J (1992) The role of maintenance management deficiencies in major accident causation *Proc Inst. Mech. Engrs* 206

Simpson G C, Widdas M (1992) Reducing major incident/accident risk *The Mining Engineer,* March, 259-265

Sulzer-Azaroff B (1987) The modification of occupational safety behavior *Journal of Occupational Accidents* 9 1987, 177-197, Elsevier Science Publishers B V, Amsterdam

APPENDIX 2   BLANK QUESTIONNAIRES AND ANALYSIS CHARTS

For ease of reference the Table numbers 2-8 of these blank questionnnaires and analysis charts are the same as the completed examples on pages 25-32.

Table 2 To be completed by individual workers

	Generic rule set	Score
1	The rules do not always describe the best way of working	
2	Supervision recognises that deviations from rules are unavoidable	
3	Schedules seldom allow enough time to do the job according to the rules	
4	There are some rules which would make the job less safe/efficient	
5	I sometimes can't get the equipment needed to work to the rules	
6	Some rules are impossible or extremely difficult to apply	
7	It is necessary to bend some rules to achieve a target	
8	The rules are not written in simple language	
9	Some rules are very difficult to understand	
10	Rules commonly refer to other rules	
11	Some rules are factually incorrect	
12	I have found better ways of doing my job than those given in the rules	
13	Sometimes the operating limits prescribed in rules are too restrictive	
14	I often encounter situations where no prescribed actions are available	
15	There are no general guidelines to use when specific rules do not apply	
16	I sometimes don't know why I have to follow rules	
17	Some rules do not need to be followed to get the job done safely	
18	Some rules are only for inexperienced workers	
19	Some rules are so complex that I lose track	
20	Some rules are only of value to protect management's back	
21	Sometimes conditions at the workplace stop me working to the rules	
22	No system exists to check people understand procedures before they are used	
23	Infringements of rules occur all the time	
24	There are incentives to ignore some rules	
25	I can get the job done quicker by ignoring some rules	
26	Deviations from rules are not always corrected by a superior	
27	Short cuts are acceptable when they involve little or no risk	
28	There are circumstances where managers will support rules being broken	
29	Management sometimes pressure people to break rules	
30	The workforce sometimes pressure people to break rules	
31	Staff shortages sometimes result in rules being broken to get the job done	
32	There are some rules where your natural reaction would be to break them	
33	Contractors are allowed different safety standards	
34	There is no efficient procedure to monitor that rules are kept to	
35	Supervisors seldom discipline workers who break rules	
36	It is unlikely that somebody would be detected if they broke the rules	
37	There are no personal benefits from strictly following rules and procedures	
38	There are financial rewards to be gained from breaking the rules	
39	I am sometimes tempted to do work that is not my responsibility	
40	I am not given regular break periods when I do repetitive and boring jobs	
41	Working to the rules removes skills	
42	Deviating from some rules demonstrates knowledge of the job	
43	I sometimes have difficulty getting hold of written rules and procedures	
44	I sometimes come across a rule I did not know about	
45	I have rules for tasks I will never have to do	
46	I have not been trained in rules to be used in unusual circumstances	
47	I often come across situations with which I am unfamiliar	
48	I sometimes fail to fully understand which rules apply	

disagree - 0   slightly agree - 1   agree - 3   strongly agree - 6

Table 3   Collation of individual questionnaire scores

Generic rule set		Slightly agree x1	Agree x3	Strongly agree x6
1	The rules do not always describe the best way of working			
2	Supervision recognises that deviations from rules are unavoidable			
3	Schedules seldom allow enough time to do the job according to the rules			
4	There are some rules which would make the job less safe/efficient			
5	I sometimes can't get the equipment needed to work to the rules			
6	Some rules are impossible or extremely difficult to apply			
7	It is necessary to bend some rules to achieve a target			
8	The rules are not written in simple language			
9	Some rules are very difficult to understand			
10	Rules commonly refer to other rules			
11	Some rules are factually incorrect			
12	I have found better ways of doing my job than those given in the rules			
13	Sometimes the operating limits prescribed in rules are too restrictive			
14	I often encounter situations where no prescribed actions are available			
15	There are no general guidelines to use when specific rules do not apply			
16	I sometimes don't know why I have to follow rules			
17	Some rules do not need to be followed to get the job done safely			
18	Some rules are only for inexperienced workers			
19	Some rules are so complex that I lose track			
20	Some rules are only of value to protect management's back			
21	Sometimes conditions at the workplace stop me working to the rules			
22	No system exists to check people understand procedures before they are used			
23	Infringements of rules occur all the time			
24	There are incentives to ignore some rules			
25	I can get the job done quicker by ignoring some rules			
26	Deviations from rules are not always corrected by a superior			
27	Short cuts are acceptable when they involve little or no risk			
28	There are circumstances where managers will support rules being broken			
29	Management sometimes pressure people to break rules			
30	The workforce sometimes pressure people to break rules			
31	Staff shortages sometimes result in rules being broken to get the job done			
32	There are some rules where your natural reaction would be to break them			
33	Contractors are allowed different safety standards			
34	There is no efficient procedure to monitor that rules are kept to			
35	Supervisors seldom discipline workers who break rules			
36	It is unlikely that somebody would be detected if they broke the rules			
37	There are no personal benefits from strictly following rules and procedures			
38	There are financial rewards to be gained from breaking the rules			
39	I am sometimes tempted to do work that is not my responsibility			
40	I am not given regular break periods when I do repetitive and boring jobs			
41	Working to the rules removes skills			
42	Deviating from some rules demonstrates knowledge of the job			
43	I sometimes have difficulty getting hold of written rules and procedures			
44	I sometimes come across a rule I did not know about			
45	I have rules for tasks I will never have to do			
46	I have not been trained in rules to be used in unusual circumstances			
47	I often come across situations with which I am unfamiliar			
48	I sometimes fail to fully understand which rules apply			

Table 4 Analysis of quesionnaire scores

Question number	A Total scores	B Number of entries	C Number of '6' marks
1			
2			
3			
4			
5			
6			
7			
8			
9			
10			
11			
12			
13			
14			
15			
16			
17			
18			
19			
20			
21			
22			
23			
24			
25			
26			
27			
28			
29			
30			
31			
32			
33			
34			
35			
36			
37			
38			
39			
40			
41			
42			
43			
44			
45			
46			
47			
48			

Table 5 The matrix analysis chart for total scores (from Column A)

Generic question set		Score	A	B	C	D	E	F	G	H	I	J	K	L	M
1	The rules do not always describe the best way of working														
2	Supervision recognise that deviations from rules are unavoidable														
3	Schedules seldom allow enough time to do the job according to the rules														
4	There are some rules which would make the job less safe/efficient														
5	I sometimes can't get the equipment needed to work to the rules														
6	Some rules are impossible or extremely difficult to apply														
7	It is necessary to bend some rules to achieve a target														
8	The rules are not written in simple language														
9	Some rules are very difficult to understand														
10	Rules commonly refer to other rules														
11	Some rules are factually incorrect														
12	I have found better ways of doing my job than those given in the rules														
13	Sometimes the operating limits prescribed in rules are too restrictive														
14	I often encounter situations where no prescribed actions are available														
15	There are no general guidelines to use when specific rules do not apply														
16	I sometimes don't know why I have to follow rules														
17	Some rules do not need to be followed to get the job done safely														
18	Some rules are only for inexperienced workers														
19	Some rules are so complex that I lose track														
20	Some rules are only of value to protect management's back														
21	Sometimes conditions at the workplace stop me working to the rules														
22	No system exists to check people understand procedures before they are used														
23	Infringements of rules occur all the time														
24	There are incentives to ignore some rules														
25	I can get the job done quicker by ignoring some rules														
26	Deviations from rules are not always corrected by a superior														
27	Short cuts are acceptable when they involve little or no risk														
28	There are circumstances where managers will support rules being broken														
29	Management sometimes pressure people to break rules														
30	The workforce sometimes pressure people to break rules														
31	Staff shortages sometimes result in rules being broken to get the job done														
32	There are some rules where your natural reaction would be to break them														
33	Contractors are allowed different safety standards														
34	There is no efficient procedure to monitor that rules are kept to														
35	Supervisors seldom discipline workers who break rules														
36	It is unlikely that somebody would be detected if they broke the rules														
37	There are no personal benefits from strictly following rules and procedures														
38	There are financial rewards to be gained from breaking the rules														
39	I am sometimes tempted to do work that is not my responsibility														
40	I am not given regular break periods when I do repetitive and boring jobs														
41	Working to the rules removes skills														
42	Deviating from some rules demonstrates knowledge of the job														
43	I sometimes have difficulty getting hold of written rules and procedures														
44	I sometimes come across a rule I did not know about														
45	I have rules for tasks I will never have to do														
46	I have not been trained in rules to be used in unusual circumstances														
47	I often come across situations with which I am unfamiliar														
48	I sometimes fail to fully understand which rules apply														
	Sum of total scores														

Table 6 The matrix analysis chart - number of entries (Column B)

Generic question set	Score	A	B	C	D	E	F	G	H	I	J	K	L	M
1	The rules do not always describe the best way of working														
2	Supervision recognise that deviations from rules are unavoidable														
3	Schedules seldom allow enough time to do the job according to the rules														
4	There are some rules which would make the job less safe/efficient														
5	I sometimes can't get the equipment needed to work to the rules														
6	Some rules are impossible or extremely difficult to apply														
7	It is necessary to bend some rules to achieve a target														
8	The rules are not written in simple language														
9	Some rules are very difficult to understand														
10	Rules commonly refer to other rules														
11	Some rules are factually incorrect														
12	I have found better ways of doing my job than those given in the rules														
13	Sometimes the operating limits prescribed in rules are too restrictive														
14	I often encounter situations where no prescribed actions are available														
15	There are no general guidelines to use when specific rules do not apply														
16	I sometimes don't know why I have to follow rules														
17	Some rules do not need to be followed to get the job done safely														
18	Some rules are only for inexperienced workers														
19	Some rules are so complex that I lose track														
20	Some rules are only of value to protect management's back														
21	Sometimes conditions at the workplace stop me working to the rules														
22	No system exists to check people understand procedures before they are used														
23	Infringements of rules occur all the time														
24	There are incentives to ignore some rules														
25	I can get the job done quicker by ignoring some rules														
26	Deviations from rules are not always corrected by a superior														
27	Short cuts are acceptable when they involve little or no risk														
28	There are circumstances where managers will support rules being broken														
29	Management sometimes pressure people to break rules														
30	The workforce sometimes pressure people to break rules														
31	Staff shortages sometimes result in rules being broken to get the job done														
32	There are some rules where your natural reaction would be to break them														
33	Contractors are allowed different safety standards														
34	There is no efficient procedure to monitor that rules are kept to														
35	Supervisors seldom discipline workers who break rules														
36	It is unlikely that somebody would be detected if they broke the rules														
37	There are no personal benefits from strictly following rules and procedures														
38	There are financial rewards to be gained from breaking the rules														
39	I am sometimes tempted to do work that is not my responsibility														
40	I am not given regular break periods when I do repetitive and boring jobs														
41	Working to the rules removes skills														
42	Deviating from some rules demonstrates knowledge of the job														
43	I sometimes have difficulty getting hold of written rules and procedures														
44	I sometimes come across a rule I did not know about														
45	I have rules for tasks I will never have to do														
46	I have not been trained in rules to be used in unusual circumstances														
47	I often come across situations with which I am unfamiliar														
48	I sometimes fail to fully understand which rules apply														
	Sum of number of entries														

Table 7 The matrix analysis chart - number of full mark scores (Column C)

Generic question set		Score	A	B	C	D	E	F	G	H	I	J	K	L	M
1	The rules do not always describe the best way of working														
2	Supervision recognise that deviations from rules are unavoidable														
3	Schedules seldom allow enough time to do the job according to the rules														
4	There are some rules which would make the job less safe/efficient														
5	I sometimes can't get the equipment needed to work to the rules														
6	Some rules are impossible or extremely difficult to apply														
7	It is necessary to bend some rules to achieve a target														
8	The rules are not written in simple language														
9	Some rules are very difficult to understand														
10	Rules commonly refer to other rules														
11	Some rules are factually incorrect														
12	I have found better ways of doing my job than those given in the rules														
13	Sometimes the operating limits prescribed in rules are too restrictive														
14	I often encounter situations where no prescribed actions are available														
15	There are no general guidelines to use when specific rules do not apply														
16	I sometimes don't know why I have to follow rules														
17	Some rules do not need to be followed to get the job done safely														
18	Some rules are only for inexperienced workers														
19	Some rules are so complex that I lose track														
20	Some rules are only of value to protect management's back														
21	Sometimes conditions at the workplace stop me working to the rules														
22	No system exists to check people understand procedures before they are used														
23	Infringements of rules occur all the time														
24	There are incentives to ignore some rules														
25	I can get the job done quicker by ignoring some rules														
26	Deviations from rules are not always corrected by a superior														
27	Short cuts are acceptable when they involve little or no risk														
28	There are circumstances where managers will support rules being broken														
29	Management sometimes pressure people to break rules														
30	The workforce sometimes pressure people to break rules														
31	Staff shortages sometimes result in rules being broken to get the job done														
32	There are some rules where your natural reaction would be to break them														
33	Contractors are allowed different safety standards														
34	There is no efficient procedure to monitor that rules are kept to														
35	Supervisors seldom discipline workers who break rules														
36	It is unlikely that somebody would be detected if they broke the rules														
37	There are no personal benefits from strictly following rules and procedures														
38	There are financial rewards to be gained from breaking the rules														
39	I am sometimes tempted to do work that is not my responsibility														
40	I am not given regular break periods when I do repetitive and boring jobs														
41	Working to the rules removes skills														
42	Deviating from some rules demonstrates knowledge of the job														
43	I sometimes have difficulty getting hold of written rules and procedures														
44	I sometimes come across a rule I did not know about														
45	I have rules for tasks I will never have to do														
46	I have not been trained in rules to be used in unusual circumstances														
47	I often come across situations with which I am unfamiliar														
48	I sometimes fail to fully understand which rules apply														
	Sum of number of full mark scores														

Table 8   Selection of solution avenues for given rule set

General avenues for solutions		A Total score	B Nos entries	C Nos '6'	D Mean score	Selection
A	Rules and procedures - aims and objectives				divide by 19	
B	Rules and procedures - application				divide by 9	
C	Training - rules and procedures				divide by 13	
D	Training - hazards and risks				divide by 16	
E	Safety commitment - workforce				divide by 19	
F	Safety commitment - management				divide by 18	
G	Supervision - monitoring and detection				divide by 15	
H	Supervision - style				divide by 8	
I	Plant and equipment design and modification				divide by 12	
J	Job design				divide by 11	
K	Work conditions				divide by 7	
L	Logistic support				divide by 8	
M	Organisation				divide by 12	

For Column D - simply divide the total scores in Column A by the numbers shown in Column D. Note these are different for each row.

Use * to identify the top three scores in columns A-D. Priority generic solutions are selected where at least three scoring methods are marked *.

APPENDIX 3   THE INTERVIEW

The interview is designed to gain general information about violations from people at all levels in the organisation. The aim is to provide the auditor with a general picture of the organisational climate and culture. This information is essential when developing improvement strategies. The interview also provides the opportunity of assessing people's differing perceptions at different levels of the organisation.

The interview is intended to apply to managers and employees alike. It should take the form of a general discussion and generally last no longer than 30 minutes. The interview should be conducted so that the interviewee is encouraged to answer honestly, without worrying about possible repercussions.

Interview questions

1   What are your main jobs and what safety implications do they have?

2   Do managers always correct deviations from safety rules?

3   When accidents occur, what remedial actions are taken to prevent the same thing happening again?

4   Have you or your colleagues ever been confused about the meaning of a rule or when to apply it? If so, is a system in place to update such rules?

5   Do situations arise where you have to deviate from safety rules and procedures to meet production targets? Will managers support such bending of the rules?

6   Which are the three most important safety rules which are not always followed? Why not?

7   What purposes do safety rules serve in your organisation?

8   Do you ever have to carry out tasks or jobs for which you are not trained? What are they and why do you have to do these tasks?

9   If you wanted to improve safety in your area, what one change would you introduce?

10   Is safe working practice rewarded? Have you ever been congratulated by a manager for safe working practice?

An outline for the interview is provided above. It may be necessary to change the wording or emphasis of certain questions to meet the particular requirements of the organisation. Answers to these questions will provide information to support the results of the checklist.

1   The first question aims to assess the employees' understanding of safety and their commitment. The responses may also offer some indication of the priorities staff place on particular types of safety. Often, staff equate safety with product safety, plant safety or service safety and do not fully recognise the implications for their own personal safety.

2   Question 2 is associated with the commitment of management to rule compliance and safety. If managers do not enforce rules, staff perceive this as condoning rule violations. Alternatively, a lack of rule enforcement may reflect poor supervision. If supervisors or managers are not familiar with the rules to be applied, they will not respond accordingly to violations of these rules.

3   It is widely accepted that most accidents are not simply the result of people acting carelessly or foolishly, but are associated with underlying causes, which may reflect problems with equipment, supervision, and rules. It is important that investigations of accidents are concerned not simply with the actions of those involved, but also with the underlying causes. Remedial actions which call for the individual 'to be more careful in future', demonstrate a reactive rather than a proactive approach to safety and a poor understanding of the causes of accidents.

4   Rules are often written by people who do not have to apply them. Furthermore, legalistic rules are often by their very nature complex and therefore may be ambiguous. It is important that people understand the rules and know when to apply them. To achieve this goal, a system which allows people to air their complaints or concerns about particular rules allows for clarification of these issues and changes to the rules, which can have the positive effect of increasing compliance. Without such a feedback system, ignorance will cause rules to be misused.

5   This question is concerned with what happens in the event of a conflict between production and safety. It is important to know whether staff will compromise safety in the face of production pressures and whether these compromises are supported or encouraged by managers. Responses to this question highlight the priority which safety has within the organisation at workplace and management levels. If production pressures are frequent, this may cause violations to become routine because people are repeatedly faced with a situation where violations are necessary.

6   This question will provide the organisation with information about some of the violations. Employees' explanations of violations will suggest appropriate remedial actions, which an organisation can often deal with quickly.

7   Perceptions about what rules are for reflect the organisational culture and management commitment to safety. Positive or neutral responses to this question tend to focus on issues such as safety, ensuring consistent practice and achieving quality. On the other hand, responses associated with the legal purpose of rules, such as management protecting itself, limiting compensation claims, bureaucracy etc, reflect a rule-based culture with negative connotations for following rules.

8   When people do jobs which they are not trained in, they are at risk. Often such actions arise because training lags behind the introduction of new equipment or machinery because of a fault in the planning. Alternatively, people may carry out jobs which they find interesting or a challenge. It may, therefore, be necessary to look at job design, or train people so that they can carry out these jobs safely.

9   This question should highlight possible improvements which the organisation can make, and which will immediately improve the staff's perception of management commitment to safety. Immediate and obvious efforts which attempt to remove hazards will encourage staff that the violation audit has been profitable and that management are committed to making changes.

10   The final question is again concerned with the priority assigned to safety. If people continually receive praise for meeting production targets or for doing a good job, this will reinforce perceptions about the importance of production. Without similar encouragement to work safely, safety takes a back seat. It is not necessary to have a reward system based on prize winning and it is certainly not desirable to have a reward system which focuses on accident rates; in this situation reporting is likely to diminish, rather than the accident rate. However, supervisors should be encouraged to recognise and support safe working practices.

Printed and published by the Health and Safety Executive   C50   6/95